# THE HISTORY OF
# CLEVELANDS HOUSE
### · MAGIC SUMMERS ·

# THE HISTORY OF
# CLEVELANDS HOUSE

### · MAGIC SUMMERS ·

# Susan Pryke

*The* BOSTON
MILLS PRESS

Canadian Cataloging in Publication Data

Pryke, Susan, 1952—
The history of Clevelands House : magic summers

Includes bibliographical references.
ISBN 1-55046-343-8

1. Clevelands House (Minett, Ont.) - History. I. Title
TX941.C53P79 2001    647.94713'1601    C2001-930110-3

05 04 03 02 01    1 2 3 4 5

Published in 2001 by Boston Mills Press
132 Main Street, Erin, Ontario, Canada  N0B 1T0
Tel  519-833-2407 • Fax  519-833-2195
e-mail: books@bostonmillspress.com
www.bostonmillspress.com

An affiliate of Stoddart Publishing Co. Limited
895 Don Mills Road,  #400 2 Park Centre,
Toronto, Ontario Canada  M3C 1W3
Tel  416-445-3333 • Fax  416-445-5991

Distributed in Canada by
General Distribution Services Limited
325 Humber College Blvd., Toronto, Canada  M9W 7C3
Orders: 1-800-387-0141 Ontario & Quebec
Orders: 1-800-387-0172 Ontario & other provinces
email: cservice@genpub.com

Distributed in the United States by
General Distribution Services Inc.
PMB 128, 4500 Witmer Industrial Estates
Niagara Falls; New York  14305-1386
Toll-free: 1-800-805-1083 • Toll-free fax: 1-800-481-6207
email: gdsinc@genpub.com • www.genpub.com

Dust jacket design by Gillian Stead
Book design by Sue Breen and Chris McCorkindale
McCorkindale Advertising & Design

Printed in Canada

THE CANADA COUNCIL | LE CONSEIL DES ARTS
FOR THE ARTS | DU CANADA
SINCE 1957 | DEPUIS 1957

*We acknowledge for their financial support of our publishing
program the Canada Council, the Ontario Arts Council, and
the Government of Canada throughout the Book publishing
Industry Development Program (BPIDP).*

*Front Dust Jacket:*
Lakeside entrance, Clevelands House.

*Rear Dust Jacket*
Sunset at Clevelands House.

*Page 2*
Clevelands House chairs.

*Page 3*
Aerial view of Clevelands House waterfront.

*Page 5*
Waterfront trail.

# Contents

*NIGHTTIME VIEW ALONG THE VERANDAH.*

# Acknowledgments

Through the course of the research for this book, I've met many people and listened with fascination to their stories about the Minetts and the village they founded on the shores of Lake Rosseau.

This book would not have been possible without the assistance and generosity of the people listed below, or the foresight of the owners of Clevelands House, Bob and Fran Cornell. They realized the importance of preserving rare photographs and chronicling the legends and insights of the older generation before the information disappears completely.

I would also like to thank Bob Shaw of Clevelands House and John Denison of The Boston Mills Press for their help. I was fortunate to have the previous research of Carol Hosking to light my path as I delved deeper into the history of Clevelands House.

Margaret Minett Abbasi
Florence Aitken
Vera Ames
Fred Barnes
Miriam Barnes
Paul Bennett
John Chenhall
Alldyn Clark
Sandy Cornell
Violet Crowder
Sean Dempsey
Betty Dodd
Susan Elms
Christine Gilley
Laura Gockel
Paul Gockel
Gonneau family

Bill Gray
Daniel Hyatt
Isabel Ingram
Audrey Keall
Helen Littlejohn
Betty Marshall
Jean Matheson
Bob McKenna
Mary McKenna
Pat McKenzie
Grace McKnight
Clint McNaughton
Glynis Miller
Everet Minett
Jim Minett
John Newton
Winsome Newton

Brendan O'Brien
John Paddon
Archie Pain
Ed Paullette
Mike Ralls
Shirley Rawlinson
Arla Rebman
Carol Robinson
Vivian Rogers
Don Street
Ora Taylor
Michael Thompson
George Thorel
Ron Turenne
Iris and Irvin Wallace

CLEVELANDS, LAKE ROSSEAU.

*CLEVELANDS HOUSE CIRCA 1907. The fence runs along the line of the 11th Concession of Medora Township, the southern boundary of the Clevelands House property at that time.* PHOTO COURTESY OF MUSKOKA LAKES MUSEUM

# Preface

*It is the constant change which affords such pleasure to the eye on the lakes of Muskoka; and though the component parts of the landscape shall be of the same —water, and rock, and tree—yet the ever-changing play of light and form constantly opens out new combinations in colour and beauty of which the sight never wearies nor the interest grows dull.*

BARLOW CUMBERLAND, THE NORTHERN LAKES OF CANADA, 1886

Water. Rock. Trees. With these simple words, Barlow Cumberland summed up the essence of Muskoka back in 1886. Prophetically, he chose the very elements that would shape the future of the district.

From the settlers' point of view, these natural features were often more a curse than a blessing. As the pioneers struggled to coax crops from the rugged Canadian Shield, it seemed at times that Muskoka was destined to fail as a settlement. One writer joked that you'd have to save up a year's supply of tea leaves to get enough soil to plant potatoes.

THE HOLIDAY GUESTS. *Once people discovered the rejuvenating properties of Muskoka, they packed their bags and came for the whole summer. These visitors are waiting for the steamer at the Clevelands House dock, around 1907.*

NATIONAL ARCHIVES OF CANADA PA163329

But fate and the spirit of enterprise intervened. Muskoka's so-called liabilities became her greatest assets. Tourists discovered Muskoka's natural beauty. The clear air and bracing waters were considered a tonic. Doctors sent their patients to Muskoka to get well, and they did.

Thanks to the water, the rocks and the trees, Muskoka built a reputation as a place that revives body and spirit. The most common thread that runs through the history of Muskoka is the realization, even of its earliest lakefront pioneers, that Muskoka residents were far better off catering to tourists than farming the land.

This is the story of how one family, the Minetts, made the move from farming to tourism, creating as they went a resort legend known as Clevelands House.

*CLEVELANDS HOUSE. Fanny and Charles Minett are sitting in front of their hotel, as it appeared in the mid 1880s. With them are their sons Bert, Arthur and Ernest. At this point the hotel had two living rooms, a dining room and a kitchen wing downstairs and eight bedrooms and a bathroom upstairs.* PHOTO COURTESY OF JIM MINETT

# CHAPTER ONE

# Into Muskoka

*Sometimes one could see whole families walking in with all their worldly goods in bundles
on their backs, or a migrating farmer, with a team of oxen drawing an old jumper that held his entire
possessions, including his family. It was a rush — a boom— a land hunger. Every county in Ontario
supplied its quota. They came from overland as well as overseas, and they shut their eyes to the rock of
The Portage and held a steady faith in the green fields that they were sure they would find beyond.*

SEYMOUR PENSON, 1910

W hen you stand on a granite outcrop and look over the jagged pinnacles of pine, it's hard to believe anyone seriously considered transforming Muskoka into verdant farmland. Indeed, early documents refer to Muskoka as the "wild lands." Officials of the pre-Confederation government of Canada anticipated turning Muskoka into a Native reserve. They changed their minds as the tide of immigration increased. As well, reports of Muskoka's vast tracts of pine attracted the attention of lumbermen. Muskoka, it appeared, was too rich in resources to leave it a rugged wilderness. In February 1868, the Province of Ontario passed the Free Grants and Homestead Act, offering 100 acres of land to anyone who would build a house and clear 15 acres within five years' time. The head of a family "having children under 18 years of age residing with him" could claim another 100 acres. It all seemed too good to be true. Here was a farm for everyone, a chance at a better life.

Advertisements placed in British papers made it all seem so easy. One simply had to scratch the ground with a stick and crops would blossom forth. "And rock was not even mentioned," wrote Seymour Penson, whose family was one of many who streamed to Canada to take advantage of the government's largesse. The Pensons and the Minetts arrived in Muskoka within days of each other, so Seymour Penson's memoirs provide a clear picture of the adventures that awaited the Minetts in Muskoka.

The trip, as Penson described it, was arduous in the extreme. After their ocean voyage, the immigrants travelled by train to Barrie, the northernmost terminus of the Northern Railway at that time. From here they boarded a steamboat to journey up Lakes Simcoe and Couchiching.

*CLEVELANDS HOUSE WATERFRONT (circa 1890)*    PHOTO COURTESY OF JIM MINETT

At Washago they regrouped and fortified themselves as best they could before joining the ragtag groups spread out along the Muskoka Colonization Road. This road had been started in 1858, following the construction of a bridge across the Severn River.

For 75 cents, settlers could get a seat on Mr. Harvie's stage line or, for a lesser fare, place their goods on the wagon and walk alongside.

Once in Gravenhurst, the settlers could again seek a more comfortable passage on one of A. P. Cockburn's steamboats. Cockburn, the head of the Muskoka Lakes Navigation Company, put the *Wenonah* on the lakes in 1866. At that time, the rapids at Port Carling and a small waterfall on the Joseph River kept his enterprise confined to Lake Muskoka. But he successfully lobbied the government to build a lock at Port Carling and a navigation canal at Port Sandfield. Both were officially opened in 1871, though the canal needed further dredging and was not accessible to steamboats until 1872. The opening of the waterway helped colonization. By 1871, Muskoka's population was 5,360. By 1891, it had increased threefold to 15,666.

*CHARLES JAMES MINETT 1842-1892*    PHOTO COURTESY OF JIM MINETT

# CHAPTER TWO

# The Lost "e" — Origins of Clevelands House

*We found Mr. C. J. Minett, the bustling, active proprietor, busily engaged in supervising the large additions which he is making to the house this year. His house is this year doubled in size and refitted for the comfortable accommodation and entertainment of 75 guests. The new part of the house is two and a half storeys high and surrounded with broad porches which command a view across the lake into the heart of Venetia, while right and left the coast line sweeps away in beautiful perspective. Back of the house the ground rises into pine-clad hills where woodland roads invite pedestrian tours and open glades to al fresco feasts.*

TORONTO WORLD JULY 14, 1887

Among the earliest to settle in Medora Township were Charles James Minett and his wife, Fanny, who are remembered today in the name of the community of Minett on the western shores of Lake Rosseau.

Charles was born in 1842 at Bishop's Cleeve, in the County of Gloucestershire, England. The Minett name is still prominent in the English village, which lies at the foot of a landmark called Cleeve Hill. The village's intriguing name comes from its association with the Bishop of Worcester, who was given the monastery and land around it as a grant in the ninth century. The area was known as the Bishop of Worcester's Manor of Cleeve—which was shortened to Bishop's Cleeve.

The Minetts' ancestral home was a large, ivy-covered farmhouse called Cleevelands Farm. It was there that Charles's father, Henry, was born and raised. He was a cooper, or barrel maker, by trade. When Henry married Maria Yeend, he moved into her house and eventually took over her father's carpentry business.

Charles was the second son of a large family comprising five boys and three girls. As a boy he was apprenticed to a cabinetmaker in Cheltenham — a few miles north of Bishop's Cleeve. He also learned his father's craft of barrel making. In Cheltenham, Charles met Frances (Fanny) White, who was born there on August 7, 1843. They were married on December 26, 1866, and emigrated to Canada the following year. They settled first in Toronto, where Charles developed a severe case of

CLEEVELANDS FARM HOUSE, BISHOP'S CLEEVE. *Charles Minett's cousin Jack is pictured in the photograph.* PHOTO COURTESY OF MIKE RALLS, BISHOP'S CLEEVE

bronchitis, brought on by the city's damp air. His physician advised him to leave the area to regain his health.

At that time the newspapers were full of advertisements about the free land in Muskoka. In the fall of 1868, Charles and his friend Josiah Callard took a trip to Muskoka to investigate. The Callards, an older couple, had emigrated from England with the Minetts.

They found land to their liking in that part of Medora Township called the Peninsula. The Peninsula is bounded by Lake Rosseau on the east and Little Lake Joseph on the west.

They cleared some land and put up a log cabin before returning to Toronto that fall. Charles Minett built on Lot 23, Concession 11, and Callard built on Lot 23, Concession 10, the former being the Clevelands House lot and the latter, an adjoining lot where Cheltonia House was later built. Charles's log house was situated about where the entrance to North Lodge is today.

The following June, Charles returned with Fanny and all their possessions. Their arrival predated the construction of the Port Carling lock. The crew of the *Wenonah* took the steamboat as far as they could up the Indian River then threw out a couple of planks to offload the passengers and freight. The Minetts built a raft of logs from the woods beside the Indian River and paddled across Lake Rosseau to the beach beside their new home.

People always assumed that Charles Minett got his location ticket from the agent in Bracebridge in 1868 when he made his exploratory trip to Muskoka. They also understood the Minetts had no children at that time. So it comes as a surprise to discover that the Minetts' land ticket was dated August 9, 1870—much later than expected—and that they had a son.

The affidavit read:

I, Charles James Minett, of the Township of Medora in the District of Muskoka, yeoman, make oath and say, that I have not been located for any land under the "Free Grants and Homestead Act of 1868" or under any Regulations passed by Order in Council under the said Act; that I am the male head of a family having one child under eighteen years of age, consisting of one son residing with me, and that I desire to be located under the said Act and the Regulations of the 27th May, 1869 made thereunder, for lot number twenty-one in the Eleventh concession, and lot number twenty-three in the Eleventh concession of the township of Medora and that I believe the said lands are suited for settlement and cultivation, and are not valuable chiefly for their mines, minerals, or pine timber; and that such location is desired for my benefit, and for the purpose of actual settlement and cultivation of such lands, and not either directly or indirectly for the use or benefit of any other person or persons whatsoever, nor for the purpose of obtaining, possessing, or disposing of any of the pine trees growing or being on the said lands, or any benefit or advantage therefrom, or any gold, silver, copper, lead, iron or other mines or minerals, or any quarry or bed of stone, marble or gypsum thereon.

*Charles James Minett*
*Sworn before me, at Bracebridge this ninth day of August A.D. 1870*
*J.E. Lount Ass't. Commissioner*

Some people waited for years before "officially" locating their property, so it is likely the Minetts decided to wait until their child was born before making their claim. This would ensure that they would receive the additional 100 acres given to heads of households with children. Charles and Fanny's first son, Henry, died in Toronto in 1867. Their second son, Edwin, was born July 6, 1870, in Muskoka—a month before they made their land claim. Sadly he lived for such a short time that his existence has all but been forgotten. He died November 17, 1870. His body is likely buried somewhere on the Clevelands House property.

Within a year of arriving, the Minetts built their first wharf. It was situated on the north side of the present dock. They also moved out of the little log house that Charles had built as a temporary shelter. In 1870, Charles built a new home that still stands today and is called Minett Lodge. Originally, it was a simple square home with two bedrooms above and a living area below.

Meanwhile, settlers to the area had discovered how difficult it was to fulfill the duties of the Free Grants and Homestead Act, which required them to clear at least two acres per year for five years. An extract from the diary of Charles Ames, December 31, 1876, gives you an idea of the cost, in human terms, of establishing a farm in Muskoka: "This is the last day this year. I am over six years in Muskoka, having come here in the fall of 1870. I don't think I have over eight acres cleared and only a small part of that is seeded down. So far, no cattle, only two calves I bought from Scott Aitkins. One heifer who will be three next summer if I don't kill her this winter, for I don't think she is with calf. Of the other stock I have. . . 11 hens, three geese and two ducks." Mr. Ames had a home on the Joseph River.

In the entire vicinity of the Peninsula, the only settler with a horse was Joseph Tobin, on Tobin's Island.

The Minetts, with some wealth and somewhat better land for farming, were able to make considerable headway as settlers. The 1871 census shows they had managed to "improve" 10 acres and acquire some decent livestock. They had two working oxen, one milk cow, and a pig. That year they recorded a harvest of 40 bushels of oats and 70 bushels of potatoes. Their cow had produced 30 pounds of butter.

To feed the livestock, Fanny and Charles cut a type of grass called "beaver hay," which they found growing on the beaver meadows some distance from their home. They carried it home on their backs.

In 1872, the Minetts had a daughter, Laura Lucy Minett. She was the third baby and the third to die in infancy. Child mortality was one of the hardest burdens to bear. Hospitals were unheard of and there were no doctors nearby. The best Fanny Minett could hope for when her delivery day arrived was the assistance of a neighbour's wife, and even that was not always available when deep snow made travel difficult in the winter months.

When their son Ernest arrived in 1873, the Minetts did not register his birth—perhaps anticipating the worse. But Ernest beat the odds. He survived. Two years later, the Minetts welcomed a second son. Seymour Arthur Minett (known as Arthur) was born on August 15, 1875.

In preparing for their expanding family, the Minetts extended their home in 1874. To the lake side of the house they added a two-storey addition with living areas downstairs and three bedrooms above.

These rooms provided the first accommodation for summer visitors. The earliest guests, according to local legend, were some British peers, Lord Lambert and Earl Baker. They had travelled to Muskoka to hunt and fish, but got stranded in the snow. They found shelter at the Minetts' home and stayed there for six months. They were the ones who suggested the Minetts build a hotel.

*MINETT HOUSE (left) and MAIN HOTEL circa 1900. Portions of the Minett house, on the left in this picture, were built as early as 1870. It was a square building at that time, with a living area below and two bedrooms above. About 1874, they added more living space below and three bedrooms above. The top right hand window marks the master bedroom, where all the Minett children were born.* PHOTO COURTESY OF JIM MINETT

It was around this time (circa 1878) that the word "Clevelands" begins to appear in records as the name of the community developing around the Minett home. Charles and Fanny had likely been calling their home "Clevelands" from the day it was built. The coming of the tourists—along with Charles's 1878 petition to the federal government for postal service—gave the name greater circulation.

Cleevelands, as mentioned above, was the name of Charles's ancestral home in Bishop's Cleeve. Somewhere along the way an "e" has been dropped. One story says the error occurred in the printing of the hotel register in 1883. But the name, incorrectly spelled, has been around longer than that. "Clevelands" is on an official document registered in 1879, and is the spelling given for the name of the post office when it opened in the Minett home on November 1, 1880.

The post office made Clevelands the meeting place for the local settlers, who by now had a much easier time travelling by land and water.

Rocks were removed from the Cut in the Joseph River in 1876. This improvement allowed rowboats to squeeze through the gap. By 1897, the rock cut had been blasted to a depth of four feet, allowing small steamboats to navigate the river.

In 1877, construction began on the Peninsula Road from Port Sandfield to the head of Lake Rosseau. Contractors built the first bridge over the Joseph River the following summer. It was finished by August of 1878. The bridge was gently arched to allow passage for boats underneath. It did not inspire confidence in all passersby, however. One young student was so afraid of walking over it that his brothers had to row him to school every day.

In the spring of 1879, the Minetts had another baby. Sadly, Ethel did not live past her fifth month. She died September 18, 1879, and is likely buried on the property along with the bodies of her sister Laura and brother Edwin.

The following summer, Fanny took a well-deserved trip to Toronto, her first trip away from the front lines of the frontier since 1869. While she was gone, Charles added a porch and a large kitchen and pantry addition with a bedroom and bath upstairs. Around the same time, the Minetts began to think seriously about Lambert and Baker's suggestion of building a hotel.

Local folklore says they were planning to build a barn in 1881, but built a hotel instead. This notion was embellished in later years by Ted Wright, who claimed the beams in the lobby of the hotel were hand-hewn for the barn. In fact, they are false wooden beams, installed in 1924 when the lobby was rebuilt. They cover steel beams that were incorporated at that time.

Charles designed the hotel and built it without blueprints, using lumber taken from the property and sawn at a nearby mill. Some of these boards, when uncovered during later additions, were found to be 24 inches wide, giving an idea of the size of the trees on the property at the time. George Croucher of Craigie Lee helped with the work. He painstakingly fashioned all the tongue-and-groove flooring by hand.

Construction continued through 1881 and 1882. The hotel officially opened in May of 1883. The original building was a two-storey structure. The downstairs comprised two living rooms, a dining room and a kitchen wing; the upper floor had eight bedrooms and a bathroom. You reached the post office, which was located in the hotel in the summer months, by passing through a doorway behind the main staircase. The hotel was situated very close to the southern boundary of the lot. The north wall, at that time, was the partition that now separates the present lobby from the dining room. Over time, further additions were added—always to the north.

The construction of the hotel necessitated improvements to the Minett water supply. They erected a windmill, about where the southeast corner of North Lodge is today. The windmill pumped water into a raised wooden storage tank. From here, water flowed by gravity to pipes in the main hotel. This arrangement was adequate as long as the hotel was only two storeys. Later the tank was removed, but the windmill survived as a flagpole for many years.

*THE WENONAH, 1866-1885. Muskoka's first steamboat carried freight, mail and passengers from Gravenhurst to Port Carling.*

## Early Neighbours

By the 1880s, life was less grim for the early settlers. Enough people had moved to the Peninsula to share the heaviest work. Neighbours pooled their efforts to raise barns and build bridges. The settlers even took time to have a bit of fun. Skating parties, for example, came about spontaneously whenever the ice froze. Skaters gathered at one home or another and built bonfires on the ice to keep warm. "There wasn't such a thing as shoe-skates then," noted Mabel Croucher Ames in her memoirs. "They were just a blade that fastened to one's boots and they were always coming off, usually taking the heel of the boot, too."

At least once a winter, the Minett boys and their neighbours put on a theatrical presentation. At Christmas, the Minetts entertained their neighbours with a sumptuous feast of roast beef or mutton, followed by plum pudding and taffy. They also started a holiday tradition with their annual weigh-ins. Each guest who visited their house over the holidays could step on the scales. This simple experience delighted the children, as they had no such weighing device in their own homes. The Minett family had by this time increased in size with the birth of two more boys. Hubert Charles Minett was born June 2, 1881. Bert, as he was called, became the boatbuilder of the family. A fourth son, Harry Cecil (called Cecil), was born March 31, 1883.

Two of the earliest settlers on the Peninsula were the Wrenshall brothers, Frederick and William. They came to Canada in 1865 and by 1866 were settled on the point where the famous Royal Muskoka Hotel would later be built. The Wrenshalls took an innovative approach to clearing their land by finding free labour under the guise of "education." They placed advertisements in British papers to lure the sons of rich Englishmen into the wilds. For a fee, they promised to teach these men the art of being settlers. It was a profitable venture, since all they did was give the men an ax and turn them loose with little training whatsoever.

In this way the Wrenshalls attracted George and William Besley of Chester, England, to the Peninsula. Once they arrived, however, they took up their own land, William on the Joseph River and George on Lot 26 in the 11th and 12th Concessions. (The Tartan House was later built here.) By 1886, George Besley's mill was one of three important sawmill centres on Lake Rosseau, the others being situated at the mouth of the Rosseau and Dee Rivers. Thomas Waters also had a mill at Craigie Lea on Lake Joseph.

Francis and Ann Judd came from Hampshire, England, to Muskoka in 1875, attracted by the promise of free land. With their eight children, they settled into an abandoned trapper's cabin and proceeded to clear the land and improve their homestead. The Judds opened a post office (Juddhaven) in their home in 1877. It was one of the earliest in the area, predating the Clevelands and Gregory post offices. Their son Alfred built a tourist resort called Ernescliffe, which held a commanding position on the headland.

The Judds' neighbours, Thomas and Victoria Snow, added a touch of culture to the hinterlands. Thomas was an artist who did paintings and sketches to supplement his income. His wife wrote a column for the *Canadian Countryman*. They built at the top of an impressive cliff between the Judds and George Besley's. Their home became known as the Bluff. Woodrow Wilson, who would later become the president of the United States, was one of their guests.

John Fredrick Pain, a friend of the Besleys, also received his introduction to Muskoka under the auspices of the Wrenshall brothers. Archie Pain says his grandfather was the "family bad boy" who'd been sent to the Wrenshalls to make something of himself. He spent the winters of 1866 and 1867 with the Wrenshalls before settling down to homestead on his own. He named his home Paignton, after a place in England where his family lived at one time.

Pain was born in Calcutta, India. His father was a merchant, later engaged in the palm oil trade with a partner in West Africa. He was a young man when he came to Canada on the advice of his physician. The colder climate was recommended as a cure for his malaria. Fredrick Pain spent his first years in Muskoka enjoying the forest and the lakes. He never really learned to farm but was fortunate in marrying a good solid farm girl, Martha Tuck. Martha had come to the Peninsula to visit her sister Charlott, who had married Michael Woods.

In 1872, Henry Wallace left Peel County, Ontario, to take work in Bracebridge. He helped build the first Catholic church in Bracebridge and also contructed the vats at the tannery. Hearing about land in Medora Township, he took a trip one Sunday to the village of Port Carling. There he borrowed a dugout canoe and paddled to the landing that is now Wallace's Marina. At the time, there was an Indian settlement on the shore. From there he followed a portage route and found a pretty lake, which he named Bruce Lake, carving the name into the side of a birch tree. The family is not sure why he picked the name Bruce but suspect it was after an ancestor of that name.

In 1878, Henry Wallace picked out two lots at the end of the lake (Lots 22 and 23) and became Charles Minett's immediate neighbour to the north. That year he brought his wife, Matilda (also called Mary Jane), and his five children to Minett. Four more children were born in Muskoka.

More Catholic families began moving to the Peninsula until there were enough to warrant visits from the Bracebridge priest. The first mass in Minett was held in the home of Henry Wallace at Bruce Lake. Oliver Gonneau and his wife, Mary, settled at Bruce Lake in 1879. Around the same time the Bissonettes, Jean-Maries and the Marcotts arrived. The Jean-Maries and Bissonettes were friends who came to Muskoka together from the Kingston area.

Prosper Marcott was a Christian brother from Kingston. He took the religious name "Morinus," now the name of the community north of Minett. A man of incredible vitality, he started his career teaching school in Mexico. He could speak seven languages. He settled first at Port Sandfield then came to Morinus in the 1880s. He built Marcott House, which became Morinus House when his niece Marcelline Jean-Marie and her husband, William McNaughton, took over the property.

Matilda Wallace's brother, William Delaney, picked the lot where the Wallace Marina is today. Muskoka was not to his liking, however, so he moved to Orillia. The Wallaces moved to his spot in

VIEW FROM THE HILLS. These two photographs, taken by Frank Micklethwaite around 1910, show the view from the hill behind Clevelands House. The picture on the left looks out to Ouno Island. In it you can see the main hotel with the original Minett home behind it. The barn that later became Bert Minett's boatbuilding shop is the last small outbuilding on the left side of the Clevelands House cluster. The picture on the right shows the view over the neighbouring property, originally owned by the Callards but in the

*ownership of the Fralings at the time this picture was taken. Cheltonia House had not yet been built. The property with the two-storey home at the shoreline is now owned by cottagers (the Richards, Godsons and Eastwoods). To the right of it is the land that became Lakeside Lodge. Wistowe Island is in the distance.* NATIONAL ARCHIVES PA132134 AND PA 155945

1888. That year, Henry died and Matilda was left to care for a very large family. Her eldest son, Henry Jr., then just 14 years old, shouldered the responsibility as head of the household.

In 1893, the Wallaces built a new house. This building became the tourist home called Balmoral. Although the building is gone, the foundation remains and is now supporting a large workshop at Wallace Marina.

The Callards, of course, continued to be the Minetts' closest neighbours. Fate would conspire to separate these good friends, however. The first unfortunate incident was the death of Josiah Callard. He was crossing the lake near George Besley's place in 1871 when the ice broke beneath him. He was pulling a hand sleigh, which stayed on the surface. Besley happened to see the accident, and ran out to help. "Callard was hanging onto the runner of the sleigh with one hand, but he was quite dead," Seymour Penson reports in his memoirs.

This left Mrs. Louisa Callard and her 16-year-old daughter, Ida, and young son, James. Louisa married again, to a man called John Melhuish. Her daughter Ida ran away with the next-door neighbour, John McKinlay, a married man with five children. The affair created quite a scandal in the small community.

John McKinlay came to Muskoka around 1870. He made log canoes, toboggans and snowshoes, skills that made him one of the most popular settlers in the area. Had McKinlay lived anywhere else but next to the Callards, he would have likely stayed in Muskoka, but he fell in love with Ida Callard. They simply disappeared one day in one of McKinlay's famous log canoes. Isaac Dovey took over McKinlay's land as a free grant, which he, in turn, sold to Michael Woods in 1882.

Woods was born in Liverpool, England, and moved to Muskoka from Toronto in 1882. He'd been a warden at the jail there and had received a death threat from one of the former inmates. He called his place Fair View Farm. This was on the property known today as Cedar Rail Resort. Later, around 1894, Michael Woods built Woodington House on the headland (circa 1894).

Some of the original settlers on the Joseph River were the Charles Ames family, and two bachelors named Dugald Headrick and William Dunn. The bachelors were good friends from London, Ontario. They came to Muskoka together in 1871. Headrick stayed just a little over a decade. Dunn quit the area early, but returned with a wife and opened a tourist home at the head of the Joseph River.

Charles Ames, a German settler, arrived in the fall of 1870 with his wife, Rosena, and young son, Charles. Ames chose 200 acres at the Cut on the Joseph River. Were it not for the Natives who travelled the river, the Ames family would not have made it through the first two years. "The Indians would always stop in at their house and bring them venison and fish," recalls Mabel Croucher

*THE FIRST JOSEPH RIVER BRIDGE, built in 1878, frightened young Percy Woods so much that he made his brothers paddle him to school.* NATIONAL ARCHIVES PA132130

Ames in her memoirs. "Mrs. Ames would give them a cup of tea, sometimes made from toasted bread crumbs, as real tea was not available."

In 1883, Thomas and Jessie Henry moved to the north side of the Joseph River, taking over the land originally settled by Dugald Headrick. They operated a store in London, Ontario, and had been coming to Muskoka as tourists for a few years. Henry, like many of the Free Grant settlers, thought he would be a gentleman farmer. Luckily, he had some younger members of his family to help him because, as his relatives would say, "He was a city man at heart."

Their home, Clover Hill Farm, later became a small tourist resort called Three Tree House. Jessie Henry and Fanny Minett became close friends.

On the south side of the Joseph River lived William Gregory, a friend of the Besleys. William Gregory was born in Shrewsbury, England, but had relatives in Wales from whom he later received an inheritance. Some embarrassment precipitated his flight to Muskoka in 1871. He was an entertaining and companionable settler who had married a woman of great strength of character. "She was one of the best types of English womankind that I have known—a bright, healthy ladylike person," noted Seymour Penson. Having encouraged him to emigrate, Gregory's family sent him a regular allowance, or remittance, to keep him there. He put the money to good use, hiring men to help him clear his land. He built a large home and filled it with 11 children. On the first of January 1880, he opened a post office, which he called Gregory. In the late 1890s, he came into an inheritance and added the name "Allen" to his surname. Henceforth he was called William Gregory-Allen.

## Churches and Schools

Around 1881, the Protestant settlers erected a building on Michael Doyle's property, on the south side of the Joseph River, near the bridge. This was used as a school and place of worship until a more formal church could be built. In 1889, Doyle deeded the property to the Anglican bishop of Algoma, and in 1891 the settlers began building a church. The Henrys recorded the event in their diary May 19, 1891, with a simple notation: "Commenced the church near the school." Regular church services have been held at Christ Church Gregory ever since. One stained-glass window at the back of the church is dedicated by the Minett family in memory of Arthur and Alice. The inscription reads: "He was for many years a church warden and their support and devotion to Christ Church Gregory and this parish was a great help in the early and formative years."

*S.S. 10 MEDORA PUBLIC SCHOOL 1916. This is how the school looked when it was located on the River Road. Teacher is Miss Dobson. Students, left to right: Charlie Stainer, Carl Ames, Ruth Stainer, Viola Wallace, Wilfred Ames, Tillie Grenke, Billy Minett, Alex Gonneau, Melbourne Gonneau, Bae Minett, George Stainer, Ambrose Wallace, Miss Dobson, Albert Ames, Abe Grenke.* PHOTO COURTESY OF JIM MINETT

*ST. JOHN THE BAPTIST ROMAN CATHOLIC CHURCH.* NATIONAL ARCHIVES PA160333

The schoolhouse eventually became part of the public school system in Medora and Wood Township. It was called S.S. 10 Medora. In the 1890s, classes were held at S.S. 10 for six months and at Port Sandfield the remainder of the year. In 1902, a new S.S. 10 was built on River Road. That school is now a private home. In 1932, a new brick school opened on the Peninsula Road, north of the Joseph River Bridge. It closed in 1959 and is now a residence.

Other schools in the area included S.S. 6 Medora, built at the junction of Juddhaven and Paignton House roads. There was also a school at Juddhaven and one at Craigie Lea.

St. John the Baptist Roman Catholic Church at Morinus was built in 1901 with the help of retired Christian brother, Prosper Marcott, and the parish priest, Father L. F. Collins. At that time, it was part of the Diocese of Peterborough. Priests from Bracebridge came to say mass once a month in the winter and more frequently in summer. The church was doubled in length during an expansion project in 1954, under the supervision of pastor Michael J. O'Leary of Bracebridge.

## By Train and Steamboat

In 1875, the Northern Railway arrived in Gravenhurst, greatly improving accessibility to Muskoka. The arduous trek up the Muskoka Road was a thing of the past. Tourists could board a train in Toronto and ride to Lake Muskoka, in

QUEEN VICTORIA ROCK. Paddlers view the natural curiosity, a rock shaped like the profile of Queen Victoria, near St. John the Baptist Church.    PHOTO COURTESY OF MUSKOKA LAKES MUSEUM

STEAMBOATS AT THE CLEVELANDS HOUSE WHARF. *By 1908 the Muskoka Lakes Navigation Company operated a total of nine steamboats, capable of carrying 2,400 people.* NATIONAL ARCHIVES PA 129954

comfort, in under five hours. The railway line ran right down to the Gravenhurst waterfront, where the steamships of the Muskoka Lakes Navigation Company waited to whisk passengers to their holiday destinations. The routes became so popular that the Northern, which later became the Grand Trunk Railway, had to schedule five express trains per day during the summer months.

Muskoka Wharf station buzzed with activity. Throngs of people manoeuvred among steamer trunks and holiday paraphernalia. Porters ran to and fro, helping passengers find their way.

The elegant steamboats, with their polished wood and crisp white livery, made the voyage to the hotels a grand affair. By 1908, the Muskoka Lakes Navigation Company operated a total of nine steamboats, capable of carrying 2,400 people.

Meanwhile, two other railway companies were laying down track on the west side of Muskoka. The Canadian Northern Railway opened its route to Bala Park Island and Barnesdale (Lake Joseph

Station) in 1906. The following year, the Canadian Pacific Railway opened its line, which ran roughly parallel to the CNR. With the railway boom came increased demand for tourist accommodation.

In 1887, Charles Minett doubled the size of Clevelands House, boosting its capacity to 75 people. An article in the *Toronto World*, July 14, 1887, noted the fine fishing available in the lakes and the superior bathing beach, with bathhouses for the comfort of guests. Rates were $1.25 per day, $6 per week, with children under eight, half price.

## Death of Charles Minett

In 1891, Charles decided to add a third storey to the hotel and build a new dining room (this addition is now the most southerly portion of the current dining area, which has been extended several times since). The most stunning addition, however, was the construction of an octagonal tower at the south end of the building. Charles chose this design to make his hotel look like a ship—a highly appropriate undertaking, considering all his guests came by steamer. While building this addition, Charles fell and broke his ribs. Complications from the accident resulted in his death. He died of pneumonia, on April 14, 1892, having never seen his spectacular new addition open to the public.

The troubling days preceding his death were recorded in the Henry family diary as follows:

*April 6, 1892:* Annie went to Minetts to get a letter which Arthur left at school on his road to Port Carling. Mr. and Mrs. Minett both sick. Mamma went to Minetts, stayed all night.
*April 7, 1892:* Frost last night. No snow to be seen from house. Mamma got home about eleven this morning. Mr. Minett very ill.
*April 8, 1892:* Papa went to Minetts. Found Mr. Minett very weak.
*April 9, 1892:* Mamma went to Minetts. Stayed all night. Tom went in morning.
*April 11, 1892:* Mamma at Minetts all night. Mr. Minett no better.
*April 13, 1892:* Mamma at Minetts all night.
*April 14, 1892:* Mr. Minett died today.
*April 18, 1892:* Hannah, Ames, Annie, Papa and Tom went to Mr. Minett's funeral. Quite a number there.

Considering the Henrys barely noted the burning of their own house in this same diary, this account of Charles's death is rather extraordinary. Clearly, Charles James Minett was held in high regard in the community. His passing, so early in life, came as a great blow to his family and friends.

MINETT FAMILY 1913. Back row left to right: Bert Minett, Ernest Minett, Willa (Stout) Minett. Second row: Arthur Minett, Alice (Stout) Minett holding baby Bill Minett, Ernestine Minett (young child), Mrs. Fanny Minett. Gladys Minett is seated in front holding a camera.    PHOTO COURTESY OF JIM MINETT

INTERIOR OF CLEVELANDS HOUSE. Notice the regatta trophies on the mantel. All the Minett boys showed athletic prowess, particularly in rowing.

Fortunately, Fanny had four strapping lads to help her. In typical pioneer fashion, she simply got on with life. Using sound judgment and good business sense, she kept the hotel going until her son Arthur was ready to take control. In addition to her hotel duties, Fanny ran the post office. It was during her tenure as postmistress, in May 1895, that the post office name changed from Clevelands to Minett. Apparently, letters for Cleveland, Ohio, were being sent to Clevelands House and vice versa. This necessitated the change.

## The Minett Boys

Meanwhile Ernest, Arthur, Bert and Cecil Minett had grown into handsome young men who were making names for themselves in the regatta circuits. Ernest Minett was part of the team that won the Canadian Canoe Fours Championships in 1895. When the Pan American Games were held in Quebec in 1905, he won gold in the singles canoe event. Arthur was no slouch in the athletic department, either. He eventually accumulated enough silver cups to cover an entire mantel.

Their father's woodworking skills, coupled with their natural affinity for water, instilled in the Minetts a passion for boats. Nothing made them happier than building a boat, racing a boat or simply connecting with the water during a quiet evening's paddle. So when private steam launches began appearing on the lakes, it is not surprisingly that the Minett boys had to have one. They bought the *Gypsy* in September 1895. It made life much easier for the Minetts and their neighbours. It also give Bert Minett a chance to figure out how a steamboat worked. A few years later he built his own steamboat, the *Mineta*, on the shores of the Clevelands House beach.

## Ballroom, Icehouse and Outbuildings

When the Minetts were trying to secure a mortgage for future expansion in 1899, they were alarmed to discover that Fanny did not have clear title to the property.

THE MINETA. *Built around 1902 or 1903, the* Mineta *was a fine example of Bert Minett's craftmanship.*   NATIONAL ARCHIVES PA163727

Since Charles Minett had died without a will, someone had to affirm that Fanny was his wife and heir. William Hanna, the owner of the general store in Port Carling, did that on June 17, 1899, in front of the assistant commissioner, Peter Shannon.

After filing this affidavit, the Minetts took out a mortgage for $5,000 and enlarged the main building, adding a ballroom on the north end of the dining room. More bedrooms were added on the second and third storeys. Later, the Minetts decided to reconstruct the mansard roof to give the bedrooms in the lower storeys more protection from the sun.

It was probably during the 1899–1900 construction blitz that the Minetts established a croquet lawn and a tennis court. The rock wall now in front of North Lodge was originally built to level out the croquet lawn. The first tennis court was directly north of the hotel, where the shuffleboard courts are today. They also had a bowling green at the rear of the hotel. In later years, this green had to be moved because the shade from a row of evergreens ruined the turf. In the 1930s, they relocated the bowling green to the spot where the original tennis court was—which makes today's shuffleboard courts the site not only of the first tennis court, but also the second bowling green!

A famous outbuilding, no longer in existence, was the barn behind the hotel. The Minetts built this in the 1890s, but found it was a bit too close to the hotel for comfort. Consequently, they put up

*NORTH END OF CLEVELANDS HOUSE (circa 1908). In 1899, the Minetts added a ballroom and more bedrooms to the north end of the hotel. You can see where the roof lines join in the photograph. The white building to the right is the original staff quarters.*
NATIONAL ARCHIVES PA67360

*RARE VIEW OF CLEVELANDS HOUSE circa 1908. We're not sure how the photographer managed to get this photo from such a great height, but it's a beauty. It shows the north end of the main hotel, and the first grass tennis court (to the right of the picture). Some haying is going on in the fields behind the courts. The first little barn is clearly visible behind the hotel.*
National Archives PA 208352

another barn on the west side of the property, where the laundry and maintenance building are today. The original barn sat about where the Clevelands House bakery is today. It became Bert Minett's boatbuilding shop.

Since a resort's reputation hinged on the quality of its food, an effective cold storage facility was critical. In the days before refrigeration, this function was handled by an icehouse. Every cottage and hotel on the lakes had one. These were usually roughly built, one-room buildings.

At Clevelands House, the icehouse was more elaborate. It comprised a large central room (where the ice was stored) and three smaller rooms for keeping milk, butter and produce. Each winter the Minetts harvested ice

*CROQUET GAME IN PROGRESS, Clevelands House.*
PHOTO COURTESY OF JIM MINETT

## Muskoka Blue

There was a time, way back when we bought Clevelands House, that the only ice available was the huge blocks of "blue" which were cut from the lake, trucked up to the icehouse and piled in, block on block, thousands of them. This did us for everything—cooling the food and meat, fish, and produce, ice for the water glasses, ice for room service, ice for the dozen and one things that we all take for granted in this modern life today.

*Ted Wright, 1967 newsletter*

MUSKOKA BLUE. *Leo Gonneau washes off a block of ice behind the hotel kitchen. The blocks of ice, cut from the frozen lake in the winter, appeared blue when the light refracted through them.*
PHOTO COURTESY OF THE GONNEAU FAMILY

from the lake using hand saws (and later an ice-cutting machine). They packed it into the icehouse and covered it with sawdust, which insulated the ice through the hot summer months. Louvered vents fed cold air into the other storage rooms, which acted very much like our modern walk-in fridges. The icehouse still exists at Clevelands House but is now used as a storage facility.

One of the first staff buildings was the house built for the hired man who ran the farm at Clevelands House. This building exists to this day and is called Telara Cottage. Another staff house was built directly behind the kitchen. It started out as a one-room cottage with a root cellar underneath. Additions were added to both the north and south side for the male and female staff. George Faith, who ran the Clevelands farm operation for many years, lived in this building. It was used until the current staff quarters were built in the 1920s.

## Clevelands Farm

In the early days, the Minetts produced all the vegetables, milk, butter, eggs and meat used at their resort. They had a fine herd of cattle that grazed on the hillsides behind the hotel. It's hard to imagine today's thick woods as open pastureland, but back then guests could climb to a lookout, situated behind the present-day Corner Store, and have an unimpeded view of the lake.

Behind Telara Cottage were rows and rows of garden produce: lettuce, beans, peas, carrots—whatever could be grown—including drifts of fragrant sweet peas. Mrs. Minett had one of the maids pick sweet pea flowers every day. "Each dining room table had a fresh bouquet on it. The fragrance in the dining room was a great delight," recalls Bill Minett in his memoirs.

The area that is now the golf course once supported fields of oats, corn and hay. In 1920, S. A. Minett purchased land on the Joseph River for more hay fields. (He later built his retirement home there. The area today is accessed by the Riverdale Road.)

---

### Ferrying the Sheep

Each spring Arthur Minett purchased Muskoka lambs from the farms in Windermere. These farms were world famous for their lamb production. In order to get these lambs to the hotel, we had a big punt. The whole front of the boat was an open pen. Dad and I would go across Lake Rosseau to Sandy Bay near Windermere and the farmers, with wagon loads of sheep, would drive their wagons out into the shallow water of the bay and we would transfer the sheep directly into the pen on the punt. Then we would return home with our load of sheep and lambs bleating heartily all the way across. When we got back to the hotel we would run the punt up onto the beach and push the sheep out into the shallow water. This flock of sheep served two purposes. They kept the grass cut around the hotel and over the summer they were butchered for meat.

*Bill Minett*

---

## Light in the Darkness

As early as 1890, Charles Minett threw out the sooty old oil lamps and introduced modern gas lighting to Clevelands House. Acetylene gas was produced by placing carbon chloride flakes into a generator and pouring water over them. This created a lighter-than-air gas that rose through a series of pipes into the lighting fixtures in the rooms. Guests simply turned on the gas jet, struck a match and the room was flooded with light. In hindsight, it seems like a recipe for disaster. Fortunately, the rooms had high ceilings and lots of gaps in their walls so the gas could escape if a leak developed in the system.

The chemical process left a white sludge behind in the generator. "It was like lime," recalls Archie Pain. "There were big piles of it outside the generator. They used that to paint the insides of barns."

Around 1900, possibly a little later, the Minetts replaced their gas lighting with an electrical system powered by a gasoline-driven generator. Lights operating on this system had a characteristic flicker, which made Clevelands House twinkle at night like a fairy castle.

## The Minett Family Branches Out

In 1899, the Gregory-Allens, with an ever-growing brood, hired Alice Stout to teach their children. Arthur fell in love with the striking newcomer. While she was in Gregory, it was relatively easy for him to visit, but when she later moved to Bala to teach public school, he had a long trek. "This proved a disadvantage in the cold winter months," notes Bill Minett. "But apparently he hitched up the horses to the cutter sufficient times so that he could persuade Alice Stout to marry him in 1902."

Up until this point, much of the responsibility of running the resort had fallen on the shoulders of Fanny's eldest son, Ernest, who was itching to do more with his life. When the Boer War started in 1899, Ernest signed on as a recruit in the 2nd Canadian Mounted Rifles. His youngest brother, Cecil, joined him. What started out as an adventure for the young men turned bleak when Cecil took ill on the passage over and nearly died. Later, they were both taken prisoner by the Boers. Their captors thought it was safe enough to leave the soldiers unattended during the night by simply taking their weapons and their outer clothing. "The Northern Ontario boys of the 2nd Canadian Mounted Rifles were not about to let that stop them from organizing an escape back to the British line, clad in just their long johns," says Ernest's son, Everet Minett.

By the time Ernest returned to Canada, Arthur had married Alice Minett and committed himself to running the hotel. Ernest moved to Montreal, where he became a design engineer. In 1912, he married Alice's sister, Willa Stout, and they moved to Toronto. He joined the Argonaut Rowing Club and raced with notable sportsmen such as Ned Hanlan. Ernest died of pneumonia during an epidemic in 1926.

Cecil lived in Montreal for a while then went into the wholesale grocery business in Toronto. He married twice. His first wife was Jessie Blong. His second wife was Katheryne (Kittie) Lear.

In 1901, more Minett relatives arrived from England. William and Louisa Fraling purchased the lot beside the Minetts, where the Callards had once located. Louisa was Charles Minett's niece, and a cousin of the Minett boys. William and Louisa lived in what one relative calls "makeshift" accommodation until 1910–11 when they built Cheltonia House and began taking tourists into their home. Today the former resort is called Manor House and is part of the Clevelands House property.

Fanny Minett stayed on at Clevelands House until her health began to fail. She then moved into Bracebridge to live with her son Bert, and was later cared for in Mrs. Goggin's nursing home. She died September 9, 1929.

The stage was now set for the second generation of Minetts to place their unique stamp on the family business. One of the first things Arthur did was to claim Lot 22, Concession 11 as a free grant. He registered his deed on October 31, 1905.

*TRANSITION OF THE CLEVELANDS HOUSE WHARVES.*
*Three views of Clevelands House show the changes at the waterfront over the course of two or more decades. The upper left was taken after 1892 when the third storey had been added to Clevelands House. The upper right dates to 1907, and shows the new wharf situated just south of the old wharf. The remains of the old wharf are visible today. The lower left photograph shows the boathouse and a extension. The latter photo likely dates to 1920 when Arthur rebuilt the top end of the wharf.*
NATIONAL ARCHIVES PA155879, PA158280, PA32224

*ARTHUR AND ALICE MINETT.*
*Arthur purchased*
*Clevelands House from*
*the family in 1904.*
PHOTO COURTESY OF
SHIRLEY RAWLINSON

CHAPTER THREE

# The Unobtrusive Innkeeper, S.A. Minett

*If you wanted to talk to S. A. Minett, you wanted to be able to walk just as fast as he did.*
*He never stopped to talk. Salesmen would come in to see that man and he'd just walk them to death.*
*They had to be in good condition to sell anything.*

GEORGE THOREL

G iven the nature of the hospitality business, you would think all resort owners were jovial hosts and fine conversationalists who loved to mix with the crowds. Not so. In fact, a fair number of Muskoka's early resort owners avoided the limelight. If they were lucky, they had an intelligent wife who could handle the people side of the business while they attended to the mechanics of the operation. Such was the case with Seymour Arthur Minett and his wife, Alice. It was not that Arthur was anti-social. Indeed, his neighbours remember him as a warm-hearted man — friendly, generous, a man who always had time for children. Although he was not overly tall, he left the impression of a big man. He had broad shoulders and a strong upper body, honed by many years of swimming and paddling. Like all the Minett children, he was a good athlete.

Although he was the second son, Arthur stepped into the manager's role when his eldest brother Ernest left to fight in the Boer War. By the time Ernest returned, Arthur had married and established himself as the head of the household. He had a wonderful helpmate in his wife, Alice Stout. They were married in 1902 and officially purchased the business from the rest of the family in 1904. They made a handsome couple — Alice with her Gibson-girl hairdo and Arthur with his dashing mustache.

Arthur made things happen on the Peninsula. He sat on the board of education and municipal council of Medora and Wood Township. As a councillor, Arthur pushed for improvements to the Joseph River bridge. The work commenced in 1912. At the same time, he was instrumental in getting the telephone lines extended to Minett from Port Carling. He lobbied against the pollution of the waterways by the Bracebridge tanneries, supported funds for fish-stocking programs, and secured a police constable to patrol the lakes during the summer months.

43

CHEROKEE TRAIL. One of Arthur Minett's promotional ideas was to call the road to Minett The Cherokee Trail. He had this gateway erected to lure people to the resorts.    PHOTO COURTESY OF THE MUSKOKA STEAMSHIP AND HISTORICAL SOCIETY

He later served on the board of the Muskoka Tourist Development Association. It was S. A. Minett who decided to put up a gateway to welcome tourists to the Peninsula. He erected a banner at the beginning of what we now call the Peninsula Road. He called it the Cherokee Trail. On either side of the gateway were panels listing the resorts "along the trail." The promotion helped lure people to Minett.

Arthur, or S.A., as most of the guests called him, also felt that his business would improve if he was on a through road rather than a dead-end street. So he gave the Township of Medora and Wood a right of way over his property to reroute the road to Juddhaven. "My grandfather thought if he put a road through, people would drive by and see the hotel and want to stay," notes Jim Minett. The land transaction was completed on June 30, 1932.

In 1917, the founding of the Bala Electric Light and Power Company ignited community interest. Businessmen, including S. A. Minett, lobbied for the extension of the system to the Peninsula. To bring hydro into the community, a certain number of people had to sign contracts to wire their homes. S. A. Minett and Mr. Love of Elgin House each put up $1,000 to get the project started. By 1922, enough agreements had been signed to deliver the service. When the power was turned on, the homes lit up like Christmas trees. Children ran home from school that day to see the wonderful technology. "It was a novelty to get up on a chair and turn the light switch on and off," recalls Betty Dodd.

Alice and Arthur had a good working relationship. Alice handled all the front-of-house operations, including reservations and dining room seating. "She was very diplomatic," recalls her daughter, Shirley Rawlinson. "She would sit out on the verandah and have a chat with the people and they would just adore it. And if someone had to be moved for some reason or other, she would sit down with them and have them in the palm of her hand. She could handle people very well."

With staff, however, she was strict and demanding. If you stepped out of line, you'd be let go immediately. Some of the former waitresses admit they were afraid of her. Other staff members found her charming. Bob Cornell, the present owner of Clevelands House, came to the resort as a guest with his family. By the time he was 14, he wanted to be a bellhop. Alice Minett gave him the job and was a surrogate mother to him when he started working. He often volunteered to do extra jobs, like waxing the lobby floors, to have an opportunity to visit with Mrs. Minett and listen to her stories about the hotel's early days.

---

### The Initials S.A.M.

My grandmother also used the initials S. A. Minett, even though she was Alice Sarah Minett. She switched her names so she could sign the papers "S. A. Minett." She handled the business end of Clevelands House. She had the head for that part. My grandfather ran the kitchen and looked after security.

*Jim Minett*

---

Guests would rarely see S.A. Minett. He presided over the kitchen, where his mere presence kept everyone in order. There was never any chatter, just the clattering of dishes and the barking of orders to the chef. He inspected every tray that entered the dining room to ensure the plates were well presented.

At night he prowled the grounds. Many guests remember bumping into him in the hallways in the wee hours of the morning. He sat in a rocking chair until 2:30 or 3 A.M., then was up again at six. He lived on three or four hours of sleep a day through the summer months, until his family persuaded him to get a night watchman.

---

### Rousted from Their Beds

On one occasion, S.A. knocked on our door at 2 A.M. He said, "Would you please move your car out of the parking lot." We had struck a skunk and the car reeked. He had tracked down whose car it was. We had to get up and drive the car out of the parking lot and leave it about a quarter mile down the road.

*Brendan O'Brien*

*GUESTS AT CLEVELANDS HOUSE. Fanny Minett is in the back row with a white brooch at her throat. Arthur and Alice Minett are second and third from the left in the second last row sitting down. Young Evan Fraling, from Cheltonia House, is seated in the front, second from the right.* PHOTO COURTESY OF JIM MINETT

## Raiding the Kitchen

It became more or less a tradition to occasionally, but infrequently, raid the kitchen after the dance ended at night. I had never, never before been a part of this activity, having been too timid to engage in such a clandestine and questionable practice. However, one night temptation and peer pressure were too great and I was stationed as lookout on the lawn near the fire escape on the north side of the hotel. Frank (a fellow guest) entered the kitchen to see what goodies were available. While I was outside shaking in my boots, along came S.A. on his routine evening rounds. We exchanged salutations while I pretended to be looking for a handkerchief, saying something like "I thought I dropped it around here somewhere." I spoke in a voice loud enough for Frank to hear in the kitchen. S.A continued his round and Frank emerged with a blueberry pie.

*Laura Gockel*

Arthur and Alice Minett had four children, Gladys, Ernestine (who was called Bae), Bill and Shirley. During their early years as a couple, the Minetts' home became the social hub of Minett. They hosted card parties and musical evenings. Arthur loved to curl and was part of the rink that won the hotly contested Excelsior Life trophy in 1912 and 1913. "No storm was ever big enough to keep Art Minett and Ed Cox from driving with horse and cutter to Port Carling for the games," said historian Harry Linney. They used their own rocks then and had to hoist them into the cutter each time they went to Port Carling. S.A.'s son, Bill, and his grandson, Jim, also became avid curlers. Indeed, many of the descendants of Minett settlers continue to be excellent curlers to this day.

## Wharves and Boathouses

Soon after he took over the resort, Arthur Minett built a new wharf just south of the old one. This wharf still stands, though it has been improved and rebuilt many times over the years. If you look over the edge of the sundeck on a clear day, you can see the remains of the cribs of the old wharves lying on the bottom of the lake. Portions of the old dock were used as a base for the boathouse, which was built to protect the rowboats and punts of longtime guests such as the Rennies, the Mills, the Farthings and the Crosses.

The large canoe dock that features prominently in early photographs came into being at this time, too. It ran along the foreshore. The Minetts put a roof over the canoe dock in later years, and

THE ROWBOAT SHELTER *was a popular viewing place for regatta activities.* NATIONAL ARCHIVES PA160343

enclosed a space at the north end for storing oars, paddles and seat cushions. The kiosk also served as a refreshment stand.

In 1920, the government sent a contractor to Port Sandfield to dredge out the navigation channel. Afterwards, Arthur Minett had him clear the lake bottom on both sides of the Clevelands House dock, which he'd rebuilt that year. This allowed the steamers to come further up the dock without their bows digging into the sand.

## Improvements at the Resort

In the 1920s, Arthur Minett built the current staff quarters and started renting out the farmhand's accommodation, now known as Telara Cottage, to Dr. and Mrs. Frank Cross of Cincinnati. Mrs. Cross was a concert violinist who brought a pianist with her to Muskoka to continue her daily practice sessions. S.A. built a log cabin beside Telara Cottage for her music studio (today, a small

*THE CLEVELANDS HOUSE BEACH. In early days the swimming beach was much smaller than it is now. Some guests called it "Sissy Beach," as most of the swimming was done at the Clevelands House wharf.*  PHOTO COURTESY OF BETTY DODD

Panabode cottage sits in the spot where the original log cabin used to be). Bill Minett, S.A.'s son, took over that log cabin and lived in it for many summers when he was driving the hotel launch.

Other notable guests at that time included Bishop Farthing, of Montreal, and Mr. Thomas Rennie, who always had a bag of peanuts in the shell, which he handed out to the children. "We called him the Planter's Peanut man," recalls Betty Dodd.

Renovations and additions dominated the 1924 season. At this time, the Minetts redid the front of the main hotel, making three smaller sitting areas into one large lobby. The beginnings of the Lake Rosseau Club took shape that year, too, when the Minetts built a dockside snack bar, today called Frac's. They incorporated a post office in a separate room at the southwest corner of the new refreshment building (that post office is now the video games room). The dockside location facilitated mail pickup for cottagers.

*TELARA COTTAGE. Dr. and Mrs. Frank Cross (standing in the gateway) rented Telara cottage in the early 1900s.*  PHOTO COURTESY OF JIM MINETT

49

# The Clevelands House Experience

Accommodations at Clevelands House could not match the elegance of the world-famous Royal Muskoka Hotel down the road. Rooms were, however, comfortable and clean. Each bedroom had an iron bed, a dresser and a washstand. A single woven mat took the chill off the wooden floors. Windows sported simple lace curtains and a pull-down blind. There were no closets or en suite baths. Instead you walked to the "Ladies" and "Gents" down the hall, and hung your clothes on pegs on the wall.

When Mary McKenna saw her room at Clevelands House the first time, she wanted to turn around and go home. "It had bare floors, an iron bedstead and a rope coiled on the floor," she recalls. "I asked my husband, 'What is that?' He said, 'That, my dear, is the fire escape.'" They had such a good meal in the dining room that night, however, that they decided to stay. "We ended up having a ball," Mrs. McKenna says. The McKennas, like many others, discovered that it was the people that made Clevelands House special. Summer holidays were more like family reunions, with guests returning the same time year after year to renew friendships.

THE JOLLY BOWLERS. *Left to right: Arthur Minett, Dr. Frank Cross, and Thomas Rennie share some fun on the bowling green. Mr. Rennie was called the Planter's Peanut man as he always had a bag of peanuts in the shell to hand out to children.*   PHOTO COURTESY OF JIM MINETT

Visitors had a carefree time at Clevelands House. They signed up for tennis matches, held lawn bowling competitions and organized baseball games, often competing against other lodges for trophies and bragging rights. Once a week, they trekked up to the lookout behind the resort for a bonfire and wiener roast. While the sparks leapt into the night sky, they sang "Let Me Call You Sweetheart" and "In the Evening by the Moonlight." "It was such fun," recalls Laura Gockel.

Masquerade nights were a long-standing tradition at Clevelands House. Guests often planned their costumes months in advance in hopes of winning. If they missed the prize one year, they'd come up with an even more exotic or bizarre idea for the next.

Clevelands House was one of the few resorts that offered horseback riding. People loved taking the horses along the bush trails, or over to the Royal Muskoka to get a haircut. For many years, Norman Dennis supplied the horses for the Clevelands Riding Stables. Riding the lead horse, he guided the others all the way from his farm in Bracebridge through Port Carling and on to Minett, where he stabled them for the summer.

Natural light for the large kitchen came through skylight windows which staff could open with ropes to let the air in. "It was a hot place," recalls Shirley Rawlinson. "I remember the chefs always had a pot of warm tea to drink to quench their thirst. For many years, we had a young chap whose job was to keep clean wood piled by the stove so it was handy for the chef. Chefs were a constant problem. Temperamental. In a pinch Dad could do the pastry."

The Minetts often employed Chinese chefs who would work at Clevelands House in the summer and in Toronto in the winter. The meals were simple: roasts of lamb or beef, chicken, fresh fish. There were no flans or tortes back then, just simple puddings and fruits pies for dessert. The Minetts made their own maple syrup, preserves and pickles. When fresh peas were on the menu, everyone had to help with the shelling.

Laura Gockel still remembers the time her father caught a huge fish and S. A. Minett had the chef prepare it and pass it around so everyone in the dining room could have a bite.

TRAIL RIDERS. Clevelands House was one of the resorts that offered horse back riding. The trails wound through the bush where the golf course is today. This photograph, however, shows the riders in front of North Lodge.
PHOTO COURTESY OF JIM MINETT

CLEVELANDS HOUSE TENNIS COURTS AND DRIVING RANGE. The driving range appears to be an innovation of S.A. Minett's during the Second World War. The second Minett barn can be seen in the background.
PHOTO COURTESY OF CLINT MCNAUGHTON

The highlight of the day was the arrival of the steamboat. Nothing stirred the emotions like the magnificent sight of the *Sagamo*, the *Cherokee* or the *Islander* when they slipped alongside the Clevelands House dock. Sometimes there'd be two steamboats at the wharf at the same time. People congregated along the shoreline to take stock of the new arrivals. The young men brazenly watched the young women and the young women, with somewhat more discretion, scrutinized the young men. Many marriages had their beginning under a Clevelands House pine tree, in a boat, or on the dock, when someone dared someone else to push a complete stranger in the water.

When the *Sagamo* backed away from the Clevelands House wharf, teenagers used to jump in and hang onto the fenders. They hitched a ride while it backed up, and released themselves when the *Sagamo* moved forward catching a ride on the wake. It may have been fun, but it was also dangerous. "None of us ever dreamed we could be killed," recalls Daniel Hyatt. "We were forbidden to do it, but that is why we did it."

Guests travelled anywhere on the lakes they wished in the elegant hotel launch, called the *Mineta*. The *Mineta* ferried people to Port Carling whenever the urge to shop possessed them, or to the Muskoka Lakes Golf and Country Club for rounds of golf. The *Mineta* was built by Arthur's brother, Bert Minett, who carved a place for himself in the history books as a brilliant, if somewhat eccentric, boatbuilder.

MUSIC ON THE WHARF IN 1934. Clevelands House was the start of many a summer romance. Kirk Thompson, the guitarist in this picture, later married Vivien Dennis, the girl beside him.   PHOTO COURTESY OF BRENDAN O'BRIEN

*VIEW OF CLEVELANDS HOUSE FROM THE LOOKOUT. Guests who climbed to the lookout rock, behind the present Corner Store, would have this unimpeded view over the vegetable gardens and Clevelands House.*
PHOTO COURTESY OF FRED BARNES

## Bert Minett

Bert Minett was just a teenager when he started experimenting with boatbuilding techniques in the family barn behind Clevelands House. With the help of his brother Arthur, he built several motor launches for cottagers (including one for John Eaton) before turning his hand to the construction of a 45-foot steamboat in 1902 or 1903. This was the first *Mineta*. He left Muskoka for a short time to work with renowned marine architect John L. Hacker in Michigan. In 1910, with some financial help from Arthur Minett, Bert opened the Minett Motor Boat Company in an old chair factory in Bracebridge.

The *Mineta* that remains on the lakes today was built in this factory. The sleek craft made its maiden voyage the day Shirley Minett was born, October 10, 1918. Arthur Minett hoped the boat ride would keep his other children from getting underfoot while his daughter made her entrance into the world.

Bert Minett moved from the chair factory to the old Muskoka Foundry on Bracebridge Bay in 1923. S. A. Minett helped finance the venture.

Bert was a stickler for detail. He never let a boat leave his shop unless he was certain there was nothing else he could do to refine it. He would have a finished boat ripped apart and redone—several times if necessary. "He certainly knew how to build a boat, but no earthly idea how to run a business," says his niece Shirley (Minett) Rawlinson. "Consequently he never figured out how much it cost him to build a boat, until he finally hooked up with Bryson Shields and he was the financial end of the deal."

Shields's injection of capital saved Minett from bankruptcy. In 1925, a new company was born—Minett-Shields.

Shields's business acumen could not stop Bert Minett from putting the best into everything— and not charging properly for it. In 1934, Bert gave up his part of the company, but he stayed around until the Second World War before moving to Hamilton. He returned to Bracebridge in the 1950s.

At some point in his travels, Bert met an American nurse called Marjorie, married her and brought her back to Bracebridge. Since Bert had half-promised to marry someone else, the citizens did not welcome his new bride with open arms. Whether for this reason or some other, Marjorie returned to the States. Their daughter, affectionately called Little Marjorie, visited her father every summer at his Ennis Bay property on Lake Muskoka.

Bert Minett died on July 15, 1966. In noting his passing, the newspapers said: "He was one of the last of the old school of Muskoka's superb boatbuilding craftsmen," a man who "knew the Muskoka Lakes and made a worthy contribution to their use and enjoyment through his faithful craftsmanship in boat construction."

THE MINETA: *This is the third version of the hotel launch, built in 1918. It took people wherever they wanted to go on the lakes. On one occasion, Bill Minett took a load of passengers to the Muskoka Lakes Association regatta. On a whim, they entered it in the "chance" race, where any boat was allowed to compete. The* Mineta, *fully loaded, came in third.*
PHOTO COURTESY OF BRENDAN O'BRIEN

## Tent Colony and North Lodge

Cleveland House's reputation as a fun place to stay put increasing demands on available accommodation. The Minetts responded in a unique way. They erected several large tents on raised wooden platforms. The tents were furnished like the hotel rooms, with cots and washstands to accommodate six to eight people. For the most part, it was the bachelors who took advantage of the tent colony, although Cecil Minett and some family friends often camped out on the Clevelands House lawn. The tents were situated behind the present-day pump house on the grassy area next to the beach.

At the other end of the spectrum were the more sophisticated guests who expected larger rooms, with private or semiprivate baths. To meet the demand, S.A. built a new unit called the Annex, or North Lodge.

NORTH LODGE: The second section of North Lodge, completed in 1925-26, included a quiet lounge, library and fireplace. The Bracebridge Gazette, August 12, 1926, noted: "Among the many improvements to Lake Rosseau hotels this year is an annex with 18 rooms with baths and large sitting room at Clevelands Hotel, a splendid addition, which, coupled to the annex erected five years ago with 16 rooms and baths, gives this splendid house facilities for handling large registrations." PHOTO COURTESY OF JIM MINETT

For the first time in Clevelands House's history, an architect drew up the plans. His name was Wendell Lawson. The Lawsons were friends of the family who spent their summers in the tents by the beach. The first section of North Lodge, built in 1921–22, consisted of eight suites. Each suite had two expansive rooms with a connecting bath. The Minetts had purposely made these rooms large but found they had trouble renting them. When they built an addition to the north end of the Annex in 1926, they made the rooms smaller and put private baths in each. North Lodge was the first building in Muskoka to use Gyproc wallboard. It was also the first building at Clevelands House to have heating in the hallways. This extended the season, allowing people to book vacations into October.

The second section of North Lodge had a lounge and library of its own. People gravitated here to read books and write letters. Alice Minett was an avid reader and her books were available to guests in the North Lodge library. One of the young men who worked at the hotel spent his spare time in the North Lodge lounge, reading his way through famous works of literature. He counts it as his most memorable summer. That year he memorized Shakespeare's *Macbeth* and performed the play as a one-man show for the rest of the staff. The building of North Lodge eliminated the need for the tents, which disappeared from the scene shortly afterwards.

## The Newtons

In the mid-1920s, the Minetts met a young couple who would have a profound influence on the future of Clevelands House. Fred and Verna Newton, with their small son, Jack, came to Minett around 1926. Fred was from Windermere, where his father (also called Fred) built a summer hotel called Newtonia House.

Verna's origins are uncertain, but her relatives believe she lived in Toronto before coming to Muskoka. She was boarding with Mrs. Wallace at Balmoral House before she married Fred. After young Jack was born, Irvin Wallace looked after the boy. "I was his nurse," Irvin recalls. "I looked after him all day long. I took him out in his little rowboat and kept an eye on him until he was in bed at night."

*THE NEWTONS. Fred, Verna, and their son Jack, pose for a photo on the Clevelands House shore in 1926. The Newtons became partners with the Minetts in the Casino operation.*
PHOTO COURTESY OF WINSOME NEWTON

Although Verna's real name was Eliza, she never used it except on official documents. She was an exotic-looking woman with waist-length hair that she wore in braids coiled around her head. Everyone loved the charming Fred Newton. Unfortunately, he had a reputation as a lady's man and that reputation got him in trouble. He left Verna and became persona non grata at Clevelands House.

In the late 1920s and early 1930s, however, Fred Newton and Arthur Minett were best of friends and shared several business ventures. In 1926, Fred Newton opened a grocery store in the Minett's ice cream parlour, which everyone called the Casino. The word "casino" was in vogue back then as a description for dance halls and refreshment stands in general.

*HAPPY TIMES. People could dance and socialize six nights a week at the Casino. "They came lavishly dressed in mahogany launches," recalls Brendan O'Brien. "The docks were so crowded that they had to double up."*
PHOTO COURTESY OF MARY MCKENNA

The Minetts, however, had actually seen a big casino in California and liked the name. They went there for the first time in 1926–27 with the Newtons. Verna's brother Charlie Gamble was a bigwig in the horse-racing circles in California, and she was able to show them around the state. Her connections later proved useful in tempting American visitors to Clevelands House.

## The Lake Rosseau Club

To this point all dances at Clevelands House were held in the ballroom in the main hotel. These were rather stuffy affairs with just a pianist or violinist to provide accompaniment. Not surprisingly, the guests started drifting to Windermere House and Port Carling, where more lively bands spiced up the night.

To stop the exodus of guests, the Minetts decided to add a large dance floor to the Casino and hire a good band to play all summer long. And so the Lake Rosseau Club was born. It opened June 30, 1928. The "cushioned" floor, installed by Morton Henry, added a lively spring to the dance surface. In fact, the whole building seemed to bounce up and down when people romped to the music.

The Newtons were partners with the Minetts in this venture and likely the brains behind it. Verna hired all the musicians and took the tickets at the door. "She ran the Casino like a martinet," recalls Shirley Rawlinson. You paid a dime a dance or a quarter for three. The dance floor was cordoned off from the tables with thick ropes. The bellhops manned these ropes, opening them when the dance was about to begin and taking people's tickets.

Banks of windows opened onto the lake, allowing a cool breeze to rustle the streamers that hung from the ceiling. "It was like a carnival, or the Riviera," says Daniel Hyatt, Verna's nephew. "People came from miles around. The *Lady Elgin* would bring people from the Elgin House. Mahogany launches brought cottagers. Boat after boat. They came dressed to the nines." In the days before liquor licenses, people smuggled their booze into the Club in brown paper bags. The tabletops may have been lined with innocuous pop bottles — but you can bet most of their contents had been subtly altered with a nip of the stronger stuff. The Minetts were "deathly against alcohol" as Bob Cornell recalls. "S.A. knew that people took brown paper bags down to the club, but Alice Minett didn't want to know. She rarely went to the dances."

---

### End of Prohibition

When prohibition ended, liquor came along. In the early 30s we had a very serious problem with drinking in the rooms. Strangers would come to the dance and go up to the rooms to drink and they'd get rowdy. So in 1931 we started to post guards so nobody could get into a room unless they were a guest.

*Bill Minett*

---

On hot summer nights, the Club swayed to the big band sounds. Trombones and trumpets torched the night. The piano player's fingers skated over the keys. The pulse of the bass reverberated through the floors and found its way into the soles of the dancers' feet.

The young college boys who played in the band boarded in the turret room of the hotel or in cabins as far away as Henshaw Lake. Many became famous musicians. There were the

Adaskins—Murray, John and Harry—who became the Adaskin Trio in Toronto. Dr. Murray Adaskin later went on to be the composer in residence at the University of Saskatchewan. Several of the Clevelands House band members later performed with the Toronto Symphony, including Frank Fusco. He also conducted the Canadian army shows during the Second World War. Joining Fusco were Vern Gordon and Joe Coll.

Other musicians associated with Clevelands House included Fred Waring and Benny Louis, both famous band leaders in later years.

John Chenhall was just 12 years old when Verna Newton hired him as a band member. His brother, Martin, was the band leader

THE BAND. On hot summer nights, the Club swayed to the Big Band sounds. Trombones and trumpets torched the night. The piano-player's fingers skated over the keys. During the 1930s, Vern Gordon's band was hired to entertain at the Lake Rosseau Club.    PHOTO COURTESY OF JIM MINETT

in 1952. There were eight band members then playing three saxophones, a trumpet, trombone, bass, piano and drums. They called themselves the Clevelands Lake Rosseau Orchestra. "We played big band sounds," Chenhall remembers: "Glenn Miller's 'String of Pearls,' 'Pennsylvania 6-5000.' It was all quite grand." The band members mixed freely with the guests. Some of them came up to their quarters in the Clevelands House turret to jam with the orchestra or just clown around. Chenhall remembers stuffing the pyjamas of the bass player and hanging them from the ceiling of the stairwell. The stairwell had windows, however, and from the outside it looked as if someone had hanged himself. Mr. and Mrs. Minett were not amused.

The Lake Rosseau Club, which was still called the Casino by most people, boosted the popularity of Clevelands House. At times there were a thousand people waiting to dance in shifts at the Club. When docking space ran out, patrons tied their boats together until there was a raft of vessels six deep. "Many people who had patronized other hotels switched to Clevelands House," recalls Brendan O'Brien, whose own family had been regulars at the Belmont House until they visited the Lake Rosseau Club one night. The following year, they booked into Clevelands House.

In the 1930s, the Newtons put slot machines into the Club. Although the machines were illegal, the police pretty much turned a blind eye. It was, after all, the Depression, and the "one-armed bandits" helped the resorts survive. Still, the staff were trained to get the machines out of the Club and into a storage room at North Lodge if a police car happened to come by. The slot machines were placed in the clubs by various operators who took a share of the profits. Harold Thompson, who owned the Clevelands House slot machines, had rivals in the business who occasionally raided his venues. After a late-night raid at Clevelands House, S.A. decided the slot machines had to go.

## The Lone Star and 21 Club

Another Minett-Newton business venture was the Lone Star coffee shop at the corner of Peninsula and Juddhaven roads. By 1928, more people were arriving at Clevelands House by car than by steamboat and they needed places to buy gasoline. Fred Newton put in gas pumps at the Lone Star around the same time Arthur Minett gave the municipality land to relocate the Juddhaven Road. Arthur also installed gas pumps at Clevelands House and had a small service centre just west of Minett Lodge.

The Lone Star catered mainly to the after-dance crowd from the Casino, who were looking for a bite to eat. The Newtons also built a few rental cabins on the property. Although Fred ran the business, the land was in Verna Newton's name. Arthur Minett sold it to her for one dollar on September 25, 1933.

The Lone Star was named after the Lone Star State, in honour of the governor of Texas who opened the coffee shop in the 1930s. The governor, like many other well-to-do Americans, was introduced to Clevelands House as a result of Verna Newton's California connections. When she took the Minetts to her brother's place in California each year, they'd meet many influential people in her brother's racing box.

Fred Newton and Arthur Minett also joined forces to build a casino in Port Carling in 1932. They got the operation started, but turned it over to John Whiting a few years later. Whiting changed the name to the 21 Club and made the place hum.

## Verena Newton, First Female Golf Pro in Canada

Arthur had a busy year in 1932. Besides opening the road past his property, and partnering with Fred Newton in the Lone Star and Port Carling casino project, he helped get the Lakeside Golf Club up and running. With encouragement from Arthur Minett, Ed Leef constructed the

*LONE STAR COFFEE SHOP AND CABINS. Named after the governor of Texas, the Lone Star catered to the after-dance crowd, who often partied into the wee hours of the morning.* PHOTO COURTESY OF JOHN NEWTON

*DAWN OF THE AUTOMOBILE. Hoping to attract more passing motorists, Arthur Minett decided to give the municipality land to reroute the Juddhaven road past his property in 1932. He also installed gas pumps and a service garage beside the Minett home. While they knew the automobile was important to their business, neither Alice nor Arthur Minett ever learned to drive. One of these cars belonged to the Minetts and the other to the Newtons.* PHOTO COURTESY OF JIM MINETT

*AERIAL VIEW OF CLEVELANDS HOUSE. This picture shows Clevelands House before the Juddhaven Road passed through the property.* PHOTO COURTESY OF MUSKOKA LAKES MUSEUM

Lakeside course on his fields at Leefholme. This is the property where Lakeside Lodge is today. Fred Newton's sister Verena took charge of the fairways, becoming the first female golf pro in Canada. Verena had been a protégé of Hughie Logan, who was the pro at Windermere Golf and Country Club for many years.

Every year, Verena would make a marathon swim between Clevelands House and Windermere House. She developed Bright's disease, however, and died very young. Her death was a great loss to the community. Her aunt, Verna Newton, always blamed the long-distance swims for exacerbating the disease that eventually claimed her.

## The Children: Gladys, Bae, Bill and Shirley

CLEVELANDS HOUSE BATHING BEAUTIES 1932. On the right is Verena Newton, who was the first female golf pro in Canada. At the time this picture was taken, she was golf pro at the Lakeside Golf Club in Minett. Verena made an event of an annual swim between Clevelands House and Windermere. She is pictured with (left to right) Betty Bond, Edla Ericson and Marg Jackson. PHOTO COURTESY OF BRENDAN O'BRIEN

All the Minett children went to private school after completing classes at S.S. 10 Medora. Gladys, the eldest, took a job at Eaton's in Toronto and married George Alport. Shirley, the youngest, helped her mother and father every summer while she was attending Havergal Ladies College. She did all the typing and often helped with the housecleaning and changeover. She married Jack Rawlinson, whose family ran a furniture business in Toronto.

Ernestine had perhaps the most dramatic life of them all. She was called Bae because her brother Bill called her Baby (imitating her name for him!). He couldn't quite get the whole word "Baby" out, so it sounded more like Bae. The name stuck. After attending Havergal Ladies College she continued her education at the Ontario College of Art. She was a rather accomplished artist, although she painted mostly for her own satisfaction. She took a course in dress design and manufacture in New York and for a number of years was a member of staff of the well-known dress shop of Joseph and Milton on Bloor Street, Toronto.

In her twenties she fell in love with Joe Coll, a pianist in the Clevelands Lake Roseau Club Orchestra. They could not consider marriage as he was a Catholic and she a Protestant, and at that time such "mixed" marriages were discouraged. "It was very sad," says Shirley Rawlinson, who suspects her sister never entirely got over Joe Coll. Bae did not marry until much later in life, choosing instead to help her mother and father with the resort.

During the Second World War, she joined the Navy, hoping to be posted in England. Instead she spent the war years in the postal service in St. Hyacinthe, Quebec (she happened to have the postal training they were looking for since she looked after the Minett post office for her father.)

After the war, she helped Alice and Arthur run Clevelands House. In 1948, in her 39th year, she married a pilot named Robert L. Rouse of Wellington, New Zealand. Rouse's job took them to California, where he flew for Qantas Airlines. The marriage did not turn out happily, and Bae divorced Robert in 1966. By that time, she had found a job with a greenhouse company in California. In July 1974, she contracted encephalitis and fell into a coma. She died a year and a half later, in January 1976. She had always been a favourite niece of Bert Minett's. Her ashes were buried next to his grave in the Port Carling cemetery.

Bill Minett attended Upper Canada College and the University of Toronto but spent his summers at Clevelands House. One of his jobs was to operate the *Mineta*. He'd get up at the crack of dawn and crank it full of gas from a pump in the boathouse. He ran the boat from morning to night taking guests to the golf club, to Windermere, to Port Carling, or wherever they wanted to go. "Some nights he even slept on the boat," recalls his son, Jim.

He knew the lakes like the back of his hand and amazed guests by piloting the *Mineta* safely at night close to rocky shoals or through extremely narrow gaps. In 1936 he married Frances Longstaff, who first came to Clevelands House as a guest with her aunt and uncle from Chicago in 1934.

Everyone expected Bill would eventually run the resort, but Bill didn't show the usual signs of interest. He readily admitted he had a lot of fun at Clevelands House every summer, until his dad clamped the work harness on him.

Once he married, however, Bill took his role as provider seriously. He started his own coal company in Toronto and later joined the staff at Dixon Coal and Fuel in Oshawa. S.A. never understood why Bill stayed at the job instead of coming home each summer. In the depths of the Depression, however, a man simply could not give up a job every six months and hope to find another one.

## Jack Newton

Verna Newton stayed on at the resort after Fred left her and carved her own niche in the Clevelands House enterprise. Neither of the Minetts learned to drive, so the functional side of running the resort often fell to Verna. Arthur put an addition on the west side of Minett Lodge, which became her living quarters in the summer months.

Her son Jack went on to have a rather brilliant career as a pilot. Verna enrolled him in the Boeing School of Aeronautics in California. While there, he was a stunt pilot for some of the Hollywood filmmakers.

During the Second World War, Jack joined the Royal Canadian Air Force and was stationed in Ottawa. At that time, Air Marshall Billy Bishop spent his summers at Windermere on Lake Rosseau. Jack flew him back and forth between Lake Rosseau and Ottawa, often taking the opportunity to visit his mother at Clevelands House. He and Bishop were both involved in the making of a patriotic war movie called Captains of the Clouds, starring James Cagney. Jack Newton did the stunt flying and Air Marshall Billy Bishop played himself in the story of a Canadian bush pilot who goes to war.

While stationed in Ottawa, Jack Newton helped rescue some airmen from the bush and became a local hero. He was promoted to the rank of sergeant, at which time Verna insisted he get his photo taken. He walked into the nearest studio, which happened to be that of the famous photographer Karsh. One of Karsh's models was the lovely Winsome Hooper, of the Rockcliffe area of Ottawa. Jack Newton saw her picture on Karsh's wall and decided he must meet her. He finagled an introduction, and was soon dating Winsome. They were later married.

## The Neighbourhood

The owners of Clevelands House could not expect guests to come back year after year strictly from a sense of loyalty. New resorts vied for their business. That competition kept the Minetts on their toes. One of the leaders in tourist innovation was their neighbour Laura Tyson McKinley, a widow whose husband had died within a few years of their marriage. He was Professor Charles McKinley of the University of Toronto. She later married Philip Graham Bell.

As a child, Laura Tyson suffered from respiratory problems and was sent to California in hopes the climate would cure her. She missed her native Ontario, however, and hearing about the healthy properties of Muskoka, decided to give the area a try. She stayed with the Minetts one winter, then in 1909 purchased Richard Gregory-Allen's place.

Richard Gregory-Allen took over some of his father's property on the Joseph River in 1903. Here he built Golpha House, a small tourist home capable of accommodating 50 people. Laura McKinley bought this hotel and renamed it Nepahwin. The name comes from the poem "Hiawatha" and signifies the spirit of peace and rest.

A few years later, she purchased the other Gregory-Allen holdings, which included a large home. Mrs. McKinley renovated and expanded this home and called it the Gregory, advertising it as a year-round operation in 1918. She ran the two hotels as one, often referring to them in advertisements as "Nepahwin-Gregory" or "Nepahwin and Annex." In later years, they were simply called the Gregory Inns.

In 1918, when the Minetts called Clevelands House "The House of Home Style and Comforts," and offered their guests a new heating system, Mrs. McKinley held out the inducements of "bath rooms, fireplaces, hot-water heating" and, perhaps more importantly, "a casino, dancing and good music"—a decade before the Minetts had a casino and dance hall.

A contemporary of the Nepahwin was Thorel House, built in 1914 by George R. Thorel. The Thorels arrived somewhat later than their neighbours. They came in 1894, taking the train to Ufford and the stage to Windermere. Thorel was another resort owner who embraced evening entertainment as an incentive for tourists. In 1918, his hotel boasted "electric lighting, running water in every room, bathroom on each flat, open fireplace and large dancing room."

Woodington House continued to thrive under the ownership of Michael Woods. His was the largest establishment next to Clevelands House, and he promoted the health-giving properties of a vacation in Muskoka. "Hay fever patients find ready relief," he noted in advertisements.

Thomas and Jessie Henry's house on the Joseph River had by this time developed into a popular tourist home called Clover Hill Farm. Their son, Morton, ran the business along with his accomplished wife, Mabel, a pianist and schoolteacher from Spokane, Washington. She came to Muskoka to teach at the Gregory school and left soon after. "Her first night in Muskoka, at the Port Carling House, she got up in the

THE FRALINGS. *William and Louisa Fraling, with baby Evan, came to Muskoka in 1901 and built Cheltonia House in 1910-11.* PHOTO COURTESY OF GLYNIS MILLER

morning and found the water was frozen in the pitcher," says her daughter Isabel Ingram. "She put her feet on the floor and thought, 'What am I doing here!'" It took Morton three trips to Spokane to convince her to come back.

As Jessie Henry and Fanny Minett had been friends, so too were Mabel Henry and Alice Minett. Mabel filled in as postmistress when the Minetts went to California each winter.

The Minetts' closest neighbours were the Fralings of Cheltonia House. Louisa Fraling was Arthur Minett's cousin. She and her husband William had one son, Evan.

CHELTONIA HOUSE     PHOTO COURTESY OF GLYNIS MILLER

---

### Working for Mrs. Fraling

Mrs. Fraling would buy all the blackberries we could pick, so my brother and I would take them down and sell them to her. One day I went in and she asked me if I could stay and work for her. It was my first job. I was supposed to help her do the dishes but it ended up that I did everything. I was a waitress and a housemaid and I helped her in the laundry. One day I finally had some time off and she said, Betty you go out and sit in the shade of that tree —and while you are sitting you can cut up these green beans!

*Betty Dodd*

---

Louisa Fraling single-handedly ran the resort. She did the cooking, laundry and bookkeeping, while her husband looked after the social activities. It didn't take long for Louisa to realize this was a rather one-sided work arrangement. She and William parted, although William continued to live nearby, in a cottage on the Joseph River.

People remember the elder Mrs. Fraling as a feisty little lady who had a wonderful collection of antiques. She was also one of the best cooks in the area — but if you asked her for a recipe, she'd leave something out so you could never quite replicate it.

Evan Fraling continued his education at Jarvis Collegiate in Toronto, then enrolled in the Detroit Institute of Technology, where he received a degree in mechanical engineering. While there he met his first wife, Gertrude. As a city girl, Gertrude found the Minett lifestyle a bit overwhelming. She often escaped to Detroit in the winter months. Evan and she eventually divorced. Evan remarried in 1947. His second wife, Olive, was a teacher who came to Cheltonia in the summer months to help at the resort.

Evan Fraling designed boats for both Chris-Craft and the Peterborough Canoe Company before setting up his own business in Minett. He was considered a genius with marine engines. He did a great deal of engine work for H. B. Greening, a famous powerboat racer. Greening also ran two long-distance endurance races on Lake Rosseau in *Rainbow III* (1923) and *Rainbow IV* (1925).

Evan moved into a new house on the Cheltonia property with his new bride, Olive, in 1947. (This house is now called Hillside House.) Soon afterwards, they opened a hardware store in the basement of their home. Evan also ran a boat livery and sold marine supplies. In the 1950s, he started to expand the business, moving the hardware store into the boathouse, then adding an upper storey for groceries, gifts and health care products. By 1957, they had built a further addition to the south. They also had a small tea room next door. (The Fraling's store was torn down and replaced with the Terrace Suites in 1981, after Clevelands House acquired the Cheltonia property.)

Mrs. Fraling Sr. continued to help in Evan's store well into her eighties. People often made special trips to the store just to visit her. "I remember Stafford Smythe thought it would be fun to get the better of her by paying for a loaf of bread with a thousand-dollar bill," says Glynis Miller, a granddaughter. "She just calmly took it, walked off to the back room and came out with his change. He nearly collapsed. She knew exactly what he was doing. There were gales of laughter about that."

Percy Woods operated another store near the Woodington House property. He was the son of pioneer Michael Woods. He started selling milk and vegetables to tourists around 1920. By 1935, he opened a grocery store, which could be accessed by water or by road.

New things were happening at Paignton House, too, although not always with the approval of the temperance crowd. Around 1918, ownership of the resort passed to Richard Pain, son of Fredrick, who had three sons of his own—John, Archie and Robert—also a daughter, Muriel. It was Archie who convinced his father to open up a beverage room at Paignton House. "It took me two years to talk Dad into it," Archie says. Getting the licence was no easy matter. "I went right down to see the deputy minister," he says. "We built it and we did a good business. It saved the day, really." When the pub opened (around 1938) Paignton House became the party headquarters on Lake Rosseau. It was for many years the only hotel on that side of the lake with a liquor license. That created a problem

*THE STAFF 1932. Arthur and Alice Minett are seated in the middle of the second row. Archie Barefoot, a longtime employee, is holding the dog in the last row. His wife, Myrtle, is second from the right in the second row.*

for resort owners such as the Minetts, who tried to keep their young staff on the straight and narrow. "Paignton House was out of bounds for us," says Daniel Hyatt, a nephew of Verna Newton. "We were never allowed to go there even on horseback. But," he adds with a chuckle, "we did sneak drinks under the table at Clevelands."

Over at Balmoral House, Henry Wallace Jr. had created a healthy business delivering people and goods around the lakes in the launch *Viola*, named after his daughter. The Wallace boat livery provided an alternative to steamboat transportation. Henry, thrust into the role of head of his family when his father died, got his captain's papers and worked on the lake steamers in 1894. Afterwards, he took a position as captain of the *Naiad*, the steam launch owned by Senator W. E. Sanford of Sans Souci Island, Lake Rosseau. There he met Mary Helen Knight, who was employed as a cook. They were married in 1901, and in 1903, Henry purchased Balmoral from his mother.

Henry's eldest son, Bruce, took over the operation of the Viola when Henry purchased the Lady Elgin in 1928. Sometimes both boats were pressed into service if the Wallaces were meeting a large group at the train station—one boat carried the passengers and the other the luggage. The Wallaces also offered scenic outings and daytrips to places such as Natural Park at the top end of Lake Joseph. Moonlight cruises were popular. "People seemed to have more fun boating in the late evening," recalls Irvin Wallace, Henry's youngest son. "They loved to cruise at night and look at the stars. Usually there was a lot of singing and good-natured banter."

Irvin's brother Edward also helped with the family business. He eventually got a boat of his own called the Lady of the Lake. Irvin took the family's business in another direction when bought a 1934 Studebaker. He started a taxi service, making runs between Toronto and Minett. He met Iris Toeppner at Clevelands House at that time. They married and lived on the Wallace property. In 1952, they bought the business from Irvin's parents and started the Wallace Marina.

Irvin's sister Viola married Clarence Ferguson. In 1947, she purchased the Murphy house, just up the road from Clevelands House, and made it into a tourist resort called the Hedges.

By this time several houses had come and gone along the concession line, including a very early home built in 1883 for the Barnes family. It burned, was rebuilt and later removed before Reg Gonneau built a new house on the site in 1920. This is the house just east of the present post office. A few years later, Roy Gonneau built a house beside Reg's for his bride, Jean Grant. (The Nicolsons are the current owners of the Reg Gonneau house; Bob and Fran Cornell took over the Roy Gonneau home.)

Minett had become such a substantial community in the 1940s that people felt the need for a community hall. Henry Wallace donated the property in 1949. The residents immediately launched a fundraising drive and had the facility open in 1951. The hall became the hub of social and recreational activities. A fire hall was added in 1958 when the volunteer fire brigade acquired a fire truck.

## S. A. Minett's Contributions to Tourism

For a man who could not drive, S. A. Minett seemed to get everywhere he needed to go. He had a tremendous influence on tourism not only in Minett, but in Muskoka as well. He worked tirelessly writing letters and organizing conventions for the Muskoka Tourist Development Association. Through his support, the first tourist information bureau was erected at the entrance to Gravenhurst.

In 1950, S. A. Minett wrote a poignant letter to the editor imploring residents to get behind the tourist movement in Muskoka before competition from other areas starting drawing tourists away. "In my opinion every living person in every locality is duty bound to support the industry that gives him or her a livelihood," he said. "Every person, every council, every board of trade, every chamber of commerce should put their shoulder to the wheel, and push, talk, give, and sing the praises of the tourist industry. Make it big, make it better. Publicity is the answer…. As the bark and milling and farms have gone, the tourist industry could also go, unless you and I make up our minds we are going to push, boost and give to support what we have, the best and only industry in our district."

By 1953, however, the physical effort of running the resort had taken its toll on Alice and Arthur Minett. Now in their mid-seventies, they wanted to retire and enjoy the fruits of their labours. Verna Newton, too, was looking forward to some leisure time. The three people who in so many ways had given so much to the hotel decided the time had come to let it go.

Although Alice truly wanted her son Bill to take over the resort, Arthur was adamant it would be sold outside the family. Part of the problem was Bill's education. He had new ideas for promoting the resort. "My father could see no reason to change," says Shirley Rawlinson. "It was two generations clashing. So Bill went into the coal business. My mother was terribly disappointed, but my father was of the old English school. Very stern." Arthur found a buyer in the person of Ted Wright, a sales rep for a Toronto newspaper who had fallen in love with Clevelands House some years before and had always wanted to possess it.

Ironically, the sale of Clevelands House did not bring the freedom the owners and their associate had hoped. Their retirement plans began to unravel. Verna Newton, who'd been ill through the summer of 1953, found she had cancer. She died in October, a month before the hotel was sold.

Seeing someone else move into the family home, the source of so many happy memories, nearly destroyed Alice Minett. She died a few months later, on January 18, 1954.

Arthur moved to the home he had built on Riverdale Road. He lived here with his children during the summer months. "I remember my grandfather lying on this huge long couch in the cottage," recalls Jim Minett. "I had to give him a kiss goodnight when I went to bed. That is my most vivid recollection of him. Saying, goodnight Grandpa."

In 1955, S.A. went to Florida after the summer season as he usually did. But he took ill. He was able to return to Toronto where he died on the last week of February 1956. In noting his death, the Bracebridge *Herald Gazette* said, "In the passing of Mr. S. Arthur Minett in Toronto on Friday, one of the outstanding citizens of the Muskoka Lakes area and a pioneer tourist operator was lost to the district."

S. A. Minett, a man who avoided the spotlight but quietly made great changes in his community, had gone. Seymour Arthur Minett left his mark on Muskoka not only in the name of a community, but in the reputation of the fine summer home that he had nurtured over the years.

# CLEVELANDS HOUSE
## RATE SCHEDULE

For Reservations — Write, Wire or Phone 16, Port C...

*Clevelands Hous...*

Minett Post Office, Muskoka, Ontario, Ca...
S. A. Minett, Owner-Manager
or TORONTO OFFICE, Suite 2224
THE BANK OF NOVA SCOTIA BUILD...
44 KING ST. WEST        PLAZA

# CLEVELANDS HOUSE

LAKE ROSSEAU

MUSKOKA

ONTARIO

CLEVELANDS H...

*Rate Card/ 1950s Brochure*

# CHAPTER FOUR

# The Ted Wright Years

*Having sold the Clevelands House to an old friend of mine of many years, I would like to tell my patrons, friends and guests of past and future years, I hope they will come again to Clevelands House, knowing they will receive the very best of care and treatment. Mr. and Mrs. Ted Wright will, I know, make a grand host and hostess and go out of their way to make your holiday a real success. Thanking my old friends and patrons for the loyal support they have given me. Please give Ted and his wife the same loyal support.*

ARTHUR MINETT, 1953

T he passing of Clevelands House from the Minett family created a stir in the community, to be sure. Apart from Arthur Minett, few people really knew Ted Wright. He had never been a guest at the hotel, though he came "from a long line of hotel people," as his friends in the media acknowledged. He was a former sports reporter and newspaper sales rep. He made regular trips to Clevelands House to firm up advertising contracts each year.

Later, in his capacity as director of publicity for the Ontario Department of Travel, Ted Wright came to Clevelands House to talk tourism with his ally Arthur Minett, who was active in his own tourist association. By this time, Wright had become a celebrity in his field and was one of the most sought-after speakers in the tourism industry.

Something about Clevelands House fascinated Ted Wright. He loved the resort from the moment he saw it. He told Arthur Minett, "If you ever want to sell, give me the first chance." It was a bold move, but one that paid off.

*TED WRIGHT was working with the Ontario Department of Travel when he purchased Clevelands House in November 1953.*

73

*STAFF AT THE SODA FOUNTAIN*     PHOTO COURTESY OF
HELEN LITTLEJOHN

Although a consortium of American buyers had offered to pay more for the hotel, Arthur Minett decided to sell to his good friend Ted Wright. The deeds were signed on November 30, 1953.

Wright was born in Petrolia, Ontario, in 1902. Following post-secondary education, he joined the staff of the *Globe and Mail*, as manager of the classified department. He then joined the *Toronto Telegram* as a sports writer. He married Laura Garbrough in 1927.

Ted managed several hockey teams and loved sports of all types. Not surprisingly, his plans for Clevelands House included the introduction of new recreational activities. One of his first innovations was the installation of small golf course in 1954. He extended the course in 1961, creating a par-33 facility called Maple Hills Golf and Country Club, which by 1968 was "fast becoming one of the major attractions in this area." He added new tennis courts, new shuffleboard courts, and hired tennis and golf pros. Waterskiing became an integral part of the recreation program.

## Modernizing Clevelands House

Wright's main objective was to make the rooms larger and give each a private bath. To do so, he had to reconfigure the hotel layout. "We went from 44 rooms down to 29 rooms," recalls Bob Cornell, who became the hotel manager during the Ted Wright years. This meant fewer people could stay at the resort. The improvements, however, allowed the Wrights to charge higher rates, so everything balanced out in the end.

Every room got a facelift, with Bob Cornell overseeing the work in the winter months. They repainted, refurbished and reupholstered. They laid down carpets, hung new drapes and strung new electrical wiring. They installed new plumbing and improved the sewage disposal facilities.

Possibly the most noticeable improvement was the addition of landscaping and flowerbeds. The Minetts' efforts along these lines had consisted mainly of beds of petunias. Ted Wright planned to make his grounds "the showplace of the lakes"—an endeavour that has continued to this day.

74

*YOUTH AND VITALITY. During Ted Wright's era, Clevelands House became a young people's place, thanks to promotional pictures like this.*

*EDGEWATER BEACH BUNGALOWS were the brainchild of Bob Cornell, who built the cottages and split the revenue with Clevelands House.*

## Beach Bungalows and Colonial House

During Ted Wright's tenure, the first Edgewater Beach Bungalows appeared. These were actually the brainchild of Bob Cornell, who was looking for a way to boost his $100-a-week salary. He enlisted the help of Ted's wife, Laura, who up to this point had not taken much interest in the day-to-day operation of the hotel. The rental plan provided a diversion. "She thought it was fun," recalls Bob Cornell. They started with one cottage (now unit 250), which Bob built. The revenue generated was split between Bob Cornell, Laura Wright and the hotel corporation.

Bob Cornell and Laura Wright also partnered in another real estate venture when they purchased Viola Ferguson's tourist home, the Hedges, in the spring of 1959. It became part of the hotel's accommodation. For a while it was called West Lodge and later Colonial House. They decided to open West Lodge all year round in 1959–60 to test the winter market.

They tried it twice and found there was not enough interest to make year-round operation viable.

A few years later, Bob Cornell took out a bank loan and built more beach bungalows—one in 1965, and eight in 1966. It was a gutsy move on his part, as he was putting his money into someone else's property. He had hopes, however, of owning Clevelands House one day.

## The Party and Convention Crowd

During the Minett era, the hotel had catered to a middle-aged crowd. Children under five were never seen at the resort. Ted Wright's focus on recreation and sports activities attracted a different clientele. At that time, the most popular place for singles was Wigwassan Lodge, on Tobin's Island. Under Ted Wright's direction, Clevelands House gave Wigwassan a run for its money. One of the first things Ted Wright did was to get a license to serve beer and wine in the dining room. "During the early '60s, this was a Wigwassan," recalls Bob Cornell. "It was a young people's party place. You had to knock on doors to get people to quiet down."

John Chenhall, a young band member, remembers one guest from Ohio who was there for two weeks and "didn't draw a sober breath for the entire time."

The Lake Rosseau Club continued to hum during the summer months. Benny Louis, the famous band leader, played six nights a week. Later, Graham Topping took over the job as resident band leader. Band members stayed in the little log cabin that Bill Minett had lived in (beside Telara Cottage).

THE CLUB. *The Clevelands Lake Rosseau Club band continued to rock the night away at the Club during the 1950s.* PHOTO COURTESY OF HELEN LITTLEJOHN

MASQUERADE NIGHT. *Masquerade night at Clevelands House was such a big event each week, that some guests spent weeks prior to their holiday trying to come up with a winning costume.* PHOTO COURTESY OF CAROL ROBINSON

In the off season, the convention crowd descended. Most of the rooms were now heated, allowing Clevelands House to accommodate 250 to 300 delegates from May to June, and from September to Thanksgiving. Betty Dodd, who had a hair-dressing salon in her home near Clevelands House, often found herself inundated with requests from the delegates' wives to get their hair done.

"I especially remember the Ready Mix convention that came in every year. It never failed. All these women would come up to my beauty salon and make appointments for hairdos or comb-outs for the next day and then nobody would come. They had too big a party. It was always a joke. Ready Mix is in, Betty, so get ready for the rush."

## Changes along the Concession Line

About a year before her death, Verna Newton sold the Lone Star Coffee Shop and Cabins to Stan and Dora English. They bought it in December 1952 and began transforming the little kiosk into a fully functioning restaurant, with attached living quarters for their family. The restaurant did a booming business, particularly late at night when the dances ended. Dora was a talented cook, and her meals put the Lone Star on the map. Stan's local bus service was also headquartered here. The building has had several owners since that time (including the Gonneaus, the Orffs and the McBrides) but its exterior has remained much as it was in the Englishes' time.

Another important change along the 11th Concession line was the construction of the Minett post office in 1969. It had been located in John Nicolson's house since October 1959 when Ted Wright resigned as postmaster. The federal government appointed Jack Nicolson as postmaster that same year.

## Ted's Almanac

Ted kept in touch with his guests with a chatty little newsletter called *Ted's Almanac*. This kept the guests up to date with renovations and innovations each year. His sentiments are encapsulated in the following comments, made in a 1964 newsletter: "We at Clevelands House get a great deal of satisfaction and fun out of operating a resort and, too, in constantly improving our plant and operation to provide our guests with better vacation value for their dollar. If we didn't get some fun and satisfaction out of this phase of the operation of Clevelands House, we wouldn't be in it, and we don't think you would be a guest here either."

*CLEVELANDS HOUSE FLIGHT SERVICE. In the 1950s, guests could expect air transportation from the airport in Toronto direct to Clevelands House.* PHOTO COURTESY OF JOHN CHENALL

Ted Wright swept into Clevelands House with enthusiasm. His youth and charisma were a breath of fresh air. His program of renovation allowed Cleveland House to remain a viable force in an increasingly competitive tourist market. But Wright could not have survived without his right-hand man, Bob Cornell. He was the key player in the operation, the man who ensured every part of the Clevelands House organization ran smoothly. In 1969, with a wife and young family to support, Bob Cornell wanted to branch out on his own. For a few awkward months, it looked like the heart of Clevelands House would be transplanted elsewhere.

*THE CORNELL CLAN. Back row, left to right: Sandy, Fran and Bob Cornell. Front row: David, Karen, Andrew and Graeme Cornell; Taron, Sharon, Taylor and Ted Carruthers.*

# CHAPTER FIVE

# Families First: Bob and Fran Cornell

*So much of my childhood memories are caught up in this place. Coming here was such a big event.*
*To this day the sound of clinking dishes reminds me of Clevelands House. I remember the mornings with*
*the sun glinting off the lake. The openness of the verandah. The uneven floors in the upstairs hall.*
*When I come back with my wife today, I feel I'm getting a chance to show her my life.*

BOB MCKENNA

Except for the late S. A. Minett, no one has been associated with Clevelands House longer than Bob Cornell. He was 11 years old in 1945 when he first came to the hotel as a guest. The hotel became a part of his life. When he was 14, he applied for a position as bellhop. He got the job by appealing directly to Mrs. Minett, who had a soft spot for him. He started work the following summer, 1949. "I had to wear a pillbox hat with the string that came under the chin. People just roar when I tell them that now," Bob says.

---

### The Bellhops

We didn't get paid. Our tips were our pay. We got 10 cents to 50 cents if we were lucky, for taking luggage up to the rooms. We also got all the ice money. We had to go to the icehouse, chop the ice, put it into a little ceramic container, and deliver it to the room. Mrs. Minett allowed us to charge 25 cents, and we would get that, and maybe an extra dime as a tip. The locks on the rooms were not sophisticated. I think the same skeleton key would open them all. Every time it started to rain, the bellhops had to take this skeleton key to every room and go in and shut the window. Mrs. Minett was very insistent that no water got into the rooms. I made $525 the first year I worked here. It was very good. I didn't smoke. There wasn't anything to spend it on except toothpaste and pop.

*Bob Cornell*

---

When the Wrights took over in the summer of 1954, Bob Cornell became a manager. Bob had planned to be a pharmacist, but Ted Wright promised to give him a year-round job at Clevelands House if he took a course in hotel management at Ryerson instead. Loving the hotel as he did, Bob found this was an offer he could not refuse. His parents, although terribly disappointed at the time, came to see the wisdom of the decision.

In 1955, Bob had the job of interviewing new recruits for the summer staff. One of the hopefuls was Fran Lees. Fran had just finished teacher's college and thought it would be fun to get out of the city for the summer. She got the job and, prophetically, recognized she'd met the man who would change her life. "When I came out after the interview, I told my mother Bob was the nicest man I had ever met in my entire life," Fran says. "Mother said, 'I've heard that before,' but I said, 'No, Mom, this is real.'"

Fran had the job of "housemaid waitress," which meant she had to wait on tables and clean the rooms. If the laundry staff weren't able to finish ironing the sheets by the time lunch was over, Fran and the others had to spend extra hours at the mangle. Working the mangle was a long-suffering tradition dating back to the Minett era. Many waitresses recall having to run sheets through the mangle in the evening. Sometimes they strong-armed their boyfriends into helping them.

To Fran, however, the extra hours seemed excessive, and she told Ted Wright so. In the past, such impertinence would have gotten a waitress fired. But Fran had a diplomatic way of dealing with issues, and she succeeded in convincing Ted Wright to change the work schedule. Ted Wright took a shine to Fran Lees, and she remained one of his favourite people throughout his life.

Fran took a teaching job in Toronto but returned to Clevelands House the following summer as a front desk clerk. She and Bob Cornell were married in 1958. In 1959, they bought the house west of Colonial House from the Fergusons and made it their home.

In 10 years' time, Bob and Fran had a family of three children: Sharon, David and Sandra. With his future in mind, Bob Cornell asked Ted Wright if he could buy Clevelands House. Ted Wright initially said no. So Bob turned his attention to Elgin House, which was for sale. He toured the premises with Vic Love, the owner, and learned about the entire operation. But his heart was still at Clevelands House. Before he signed the papers, he decided to ask Ted Wright one more time. He and Fran flew down to Fort Lauderdale, where the Wrights spent their winters, and told them their plans.

The next day, the Wrights agreed to sell. They realized they couldn't run the resort without the Cornells. Bob and Fran took over ownership of Clevelands House on November 5, 1969. As part of the deal, the Wrights were allowed to live at Clevelands House. They kept an apartment in Minett Lodge and also purchased one of the newer waterfront cottages. Ted Wright died in 1975, Laura, in the 1980s.

The first challenge facing the Cornells was a major renovation of the physical plant, which had deteriorated quite badly during the Wrights' last years at the resort. Bob Cornell started working as fast as he could, beginning with the upper floor of North Lodge. In 1970, he got a full liquor licence for the dance hall and dining room. In 1971, he built eight new cottages and put air conditioning into the dining room and first floor of the main hotel. In succeeding years, he added more cottages, a swimming pool, and a dozen or more tennis courts until they totalled 16 in number.

He had predicted, correctly, that tennis was on the rise, and he made sure there were enough courts for everyone. Even so, there were times when people had to book a day in advance just to get court time.

They had a setback in 1976 when a fire effectively wiped out the kitchen, just days before the summer season began. It was June 12, a Thursday. An oven overheated and set fire to the studs in the adjoining office wall. Smoke filled the kitchen and the dining room. The staff rallied and, with a makeshift arrangement, were able to feed their convention guests in the Club. The next day, Bob Cornell could not

*FRAN LEES, now Fran Cornell, came to Clevelands House as a waitress in 1955.* PHOTO COURTESY OF HELEN LITTLEJOHN

believe his eyes. "There were 12 people with hammers and nails volunteering to help get us back in order. They stayed until we were operational again," he says.

Things were back on track in 1978, at which time they reconstructed the entire Maple Hills Golf Course, building wider fairways and better greens.

Perhaps the most important change the Cornells made was the shift from a singles resort to a family resort. When they catered to both, they found the singles kept the families awake at night—and Bob Cornell no longer relished knocking on doors in the early hours of the morning.

Bob and Fran decided to take the plunge. "We felt very comfortable with the decision, because the property lends itself to families with all the facilities that it has," notes Fran Cornell. "The pool was one of the first things we did. We found that people loved to sit around it."

Today they have four swimming pools, one for adults and three for children. Their original adventure playground, built in 1989, has been updated twice. It now encompasses an entire acre and is anchored by the impressive Cleve's Fun Ship, a steamship-shaped play apparatus.

In any given week in the summer, there can be as many as 185 to 195 children under the age of 12 staying at the resort. "We have 54 people hired that do nothing but look after children," notes Bob Cornell.

*CLEVELANDS HOUSE GATEWAY*   PHOTO COURTESY OF RON TURENNE

Along with the compulsory TV, telephone and mini refrigerator, each room now has a double jack installation for computers with modems. For the convention crowd, there's a barbecue pavilion, a state-of-the-art fitness facility and a challenge high-ropes course, which is a great resource for team-building. In 1995, the opening of the magnificent Segwun Room meant the Cornells could comfortably seat 540 people in their dining room. That's three times the number that Arthur and Alice Minett hosted in the 1940s. (The staff can be thankful they do not have to shell fresh peas!)

*THE SEGWUN ROOM AND FITNESS CENTRE make Clevelands House a popular conference centre.*

*CLEVE'S PLAYWORLD. At any given time there can be as many as 185 to 195 children under the age of 12 staying at the resort.*

In embracing the future, however, the Cornells have had to let go of a few things from the past. With regret, they tore down the stables in 1977 and discontinued the Wednesday night masquerades in 1987 when only four out of 200 guests dressed up for the occasion. That same year, the Cornells decided the time had come to relax the dining-room dress code, particularly the "jacket and tie" tradition for men. Men who wore jackets and ties to work every day simply did not want to wear them on vacation.

Old friends, too, were passing away. In 1996 alone, the Cornells lost three former employees who had been wonderful supporters. Bruce Oldham, their greenskeeper, died suddenly in August. You will see a dedication in his honour on the seventh tee of the golf course. He rebuilt it entirely just before his death.

Marg Stapleton died of cancer in October of 1996. She was Bob Cornell's managerial assistant in the Ted Wright era and continued working at the resort for almost 30 years.

Finally, one of the Cornells' favourite people, Jack Nicolson, died in November with a brain tumour. Jack, who had retired five years earlier, had headed up the maintenance and building departments for 32 years. He lived next door to the Cornell family and was like a second father to their children. "Jack could do anything," recalls Fran Cornell. "He was an electrician, a carpenter. A mild, gentle man.

*SUMMER NIGHTS ON THE VERANDAH. Clevelands House has always been famous for its spacious verandahs, where people gather to read books, share a before-dinner drink, or simply enjoy the view.*

When Bob and I had the chance to buy Clevelands House, the Nicolsons offered to mortgage their house to help. How many people would do that?"

## Cheltonia House Property

Mrs. Fraling Sr. gradually closed parts of her tourist business as she grew older, until finally only a few of the cottages were rented. Around 1969, Evan Fraling closed his store. It sat idle for a few years until finally, in October 1980, the Cornells bought the entire property. It comprised 15 acres, including the old Cheltonia House, the store, Evan Fraling's home and several small cottages, including the one that was rented to the ski school instructors.

The Cornells had the old ski school cottage gutted and rebuilt (it is now Cheltonia Cottage). The store became the Terrace Suites, while the former Cheltonia House became the Manor House. As years progressed, more Terrace Suites were added and, in 1985, the elegant new reception area and lobby was built on the Cheltonia property. At that time, the former office was converted into a gift shop.

*AERIAL VIEW OF CLEVELANDS HOUSE showing the golf and tennis facilities.*

*THE SWIMMING POOL. The addition of a swimming pool was a popular move that helped make Clevelands House a successful family resort.*

## Ski School

The idols of summer, hands down, were the ski school boys. Bronzed by the sun and burnished by the water, they melted the hearts of many a young Clevelands House guest and set the standard by which all young men would be judged on the docks. Your passport to popularity was your ability to carve a curtain of spray — to lean close enough to the water to kiss it.

Many a summer romance started on the ski school dock. Shiny boats zipped in and out with guests, bringing some their moments of glory, and others an ignoble dunking.

Bob McKenna was one of the guests who learned to ski at Clevelands House. When he returns today, it's the smell of the docks — that whiff of gasoline, wet wood, and suntan lotion— that fills him with nostalgia. "For my sisters, these ski instructors were gods."

Local girls, too, congregated at the docks. "We met the greatest guys there," admits Susan Elms. "That's why we went. To flirt."

About seven different sets of ski school entrepreneurs have come and gone at Clevelands House—most of them working their way through university. The Bose Brothers were the first to operate a ski school at Clevelands House in the latter half of the 1960s. Then Don West and his crew launched Summer Waterski Services. Don Lang took over in 1977 and ran Summer Waterski with the help of Steve Jarrett, John MacDonald and Peter Herbert. In 1985, John Paddon and Gord Cook took the business to a new level with the creation of Muskoka Waterski. In addition to the skiing instruction, they ran ski shows at the several local resorts, including Clevelands House. Their company survived until 1989.

*THE SKI SCHOOL has made the Clevelands House dock the most popular gathering spot on the lakes.*

*CLEVELANDS HOUSE BEACH.*

*THE DINING EXPERIENCE. There was a time not too long ago that a strict dress code was in force in the Clevelands House dining room. In 1987, the Cornells realized they had to "bend with the times and give up part of the century-old tradition." Today, "dressy casual" is the watchword for guests.*

*CHEF HENRY MARCAN has been a fixture at Clevelands House for over two decades.*

Dave Brandstetter operated a ski school through to the mid-1990s, and today it is Phil Harding's Summer Watersports that continues the tradition of ski instruction at Clevelands House.

## Celebrities

With its active waterfront, a great snack bar and a licensed sundeck, Clevelands House is a popular pit stop for cottagers through the summer. If you hang around long enough, you may even see some of the celebrities who now make Muskoka their summer home.

Goldie Hawn, Kurt Russell, Steven Spielberg, Mel Gibson and Tom Hanks have all been spotted at Clevelands House. For the most part, people respect their privacy, although on one occasion Tom Hanks was mobbed for photographs by hotel guests. Emmy Award–winner Jane Seymour booked into Clevelands House for five days with her twins. "We've had Rachel Welch, Lindsay Wagner and one of the Maguire sisters—that's going back," Bob Cornell jokes. In 1983, a movie called *Martin's Day* was filmed in the area. The stars, including Richard Harris, Justin Henry and James Coburn, stayed at Clevelands House that week.

Perhaps the most reluctant celebrity was rocket scientist Werner von Braun, who moved to Huntsville, Alabama, after the Second World War to help the United States develop guided missiles and the *Saturn V* rocket that helped put a man on the moon. "He booked through a travel agent," recalls Bob Cornell. "The travel agent said he was very concerned that his identity be kept quiet." So the staff were instructed to leave him alone. However, there was a dress code for the dining room then. Men were supposed to wear a suit jacket and tie. Mr. von Braun insisted on wearing a bright red lumberjack shirt and he stuck out like a sore thumb. "With anyone else, we would say, 'Sir, could you wear a jacket?'" says Bob Cornell. "But the girls at the door were frightened to tell him. So he drew attention to himself. But he didn't seem to mind it."

## The More Things Change…

If the spirits of Arthur and Alice Minett still hover over Clevelands House, they would likely be reassured that the Cornells have taken a page or two from their

THE CLEVELANDS HOUSE FOUNTAIN.

management book. For it is Fran, like Alice, who handles the front of house and dining room, and Bob, like Arthur, who makes sure everything is running smoothly behind the scenes.

They are assisted in their efforts by their family. Sharon and her husband, Ted Carruthers, along with Sandy Cornell, are taking on more and more responsibility. The torch is being passed to the next generation.

The ghosts would find comfort, too, in the fact that the resort is still in family hands—not Minett hands, that's true, but family hands nonetheless. In an era of corporate ownership, a family resort is unique. As the Minetts did before them, the Cornells bring a stability and consistency to the resort experience. People count on them to maintain a certain standard. They are never disappointed. They teach their staff to be an extension of themselves — to treat each guest as they think the Cornells would treat them. Clevelands House now takes considerably more guests than it used to, but each and every one of them is still considered a house guest in the Cornell home.

If Charles and Fanny Minett could somehow return to the homestead they carved in the bush, they would surely stagger in amazement. Gone are the cattle that grazed on the hill. Gone are the banks of sweet peas that perfumed the night. An entire village of cottages has grown up where hay fields once flourished. The beach is as broad and playful as its counterparts on the ocean.

But the characteristic octagonal tower that defined Clevelands House in the 1880s still rises beyond the stone gate. Expanded and extended as it is, Clevelands House is, at its heart, the same hotel it's always been.

*NIGHTTIME VIEW OF THE CLEVELANDS HOUSE TOWER. During the big band era, band members stayed in the upper floor of the tower.*

# Appendix

## Chronological History of Clevelands House

1842   Charles James Minett born, Bishop's Cleeve, England.

1843   Fanny White born Cheltenham, England.

1866   Charles Minett married Fanny (Frances) White.

1867   Charles and Fanny Minett emigrated from England. Lived in Toronto.

1868   Charles Minett makes exploratory trip to Muskoka. Builds log cabin.

1869   Charles and Fanny arrived in Muskoka.

1870   Charles Minett gets land ticket for Lots 21 and 23, Concession 11, Medora Township.

1870   Minett House built.

1870   First dock built, of crib construction.

1874   Minett house enlarged, guests start to arrive.

1880   Post office established, called Clevelands.

1880   Further additions to Minett House.

1881   Construction begins on main hotel.

1883   Main hotel opens.

1884   Charles Minett buys water lot (3.5 acres) from Crown.

1884   Charles Minett takes title to Lots 21 and 23, Concession 11, Medora Township.

1887   Additions to the main hotel, doubling occupancy to 75.

1890   Pile dock built on location of the present dock.

1891   Addition of third storey, tower and original portion of present dining room.

1892   Charles Minett dies.

1895   Post office name changed from Clevelands to Minett.

1895   Minetts purchase a steamboat called *Gypsy*.

1899   Ballroom addition, croquet lawns, tennis court.

1901   William and Louisa Fraling arrive in Minett.

1902   Seymour Arthur Minett marries Alice Stout.

1902–03 Bert Minett builds steam launch *Mineta*.

1904   Arthur Minett buys Clevelands House.

1905   Arthur Minett takes title to Lot 22, Concession 11, Medora Township.

1910–11 Fralings build Cheltonia House.

1918   The second *Mineta* built.

1920   Dock rebuilt and bottom dredged.

1921–22 Annex, or North Lodge built.

1922   First cars at Clevelands House.

1924   Remodelled lobby, extended dining room, built first part of Casino.

1926   Addition to North Lodge, grocery store in Casino.

1928   Extension to Casino, opens in June as Lake Rosseau Club.

1929   Fanny Minett dies.

1932   Arthur Minett gives land for road across his property.

1949   Bob Cornell a bellhop at Clevelands House.

1953   Ted and Laura Wright buy Clevelands House.

1954   Building of first golf course, Bob Cornell manager at resort.

1954   Alice Minett dies.

1955   Fran Lees hired as a waitress.

1956   Arthur Minett dies, front of Minett house changed.

1958   Bob Cornell marries Fran Lees.

1959   Bob Cornell and Laura Wright buy the Hedges.

1960   Hedges open for winter vacation (for two years only).

1961   New golf course.

1962   Third tennis court added. New stables. Playground at the beach.

1963   Kitchen rebuilt. Main hotel renovated. Stables enlarged.

1964   North Lodge renovated. Beams fixed in the Club.

1965   New office, fountain moved, minimum wage 75 cents an hour. Bungalow built at beach.

1966   Private bath in all main hotel rooms. Colonial House renovated. Eight Edgewater Beach Bungalows built.

1967   Gatehouse added for senior staff.

1968   Twister destroys shelter at end of dock and damages two cottages. New entrance from dock to club and sundeck. Golf course changed.

| | |
|---|---|
| 1969 | Bob and Fran Cornell buy Clevelands House. |
| 1970 | Full liquor license for hotel. |
| 1971 | Five new cottages and three new bungalows. Air conditioning in dining room and first floor of hotel. |
| 1972 | Heated swimming pool added, two new tennis courts, two new shuffleboard courts, improvements to golf course, new pro shop. Bill Minett's old log cabin torn down. Former pro shop converted to Fairway Cottage. |
| 1973 | Every room in main hotel remodelled. |
| 1974 | Dining room enlarged. |
| 1975 | Ted Wright dies. Eight more bungalows at beach, two more tennis courts. |
| 1976 | Four more tennis courts, two badminton courts, air conditioning in Minett Lodge. |
| 1977 | Stables torn down. Storage shed completed. Former Wrights' quarters in Minett Lodge renovated. |
| 1978 | Six more tennis courts. Golf course rebuilt. Construction on dock. |
| 1979 | Golf course finished. Front of main hotel rebuilt. Staff of 140. |
| 1980 | Cornells buy Cheltonia House property. |
| 1981 | Segwun sailed the Muskoka lakes after almost 30 years' absence. Terrace Suites built. Cheltonia House (Manor House) renovated. Bake shop built. Large addition to the Club. |
| 1984 | Two hot tubs, nursery added to Minett House. |
| 1985 | New office complex on former Cheltonia property. Three new Terrace Suites. Barbecue area. Sharon Cornell marries Ted Carruthers. |
| 1986 | New addition to west side of dining room. Three new Terrace Suites. Three Hillside Suites. Bake house doubled in size. Staff of 200. |
| 1987 | New swimming pool for children. Woodside suites. TV in every room. Improved beach area. No masquerade nights. Dress code relaxed. |
| 1988 | Complete renovation of main kitchen. Now accommodating 450 people. History book written by Carol Hosking. |
| 1989 | Play World constructed to keep up to 150 children happy. |
| 1991 | New play equipment. Baseball field completed. Walking/jogging trails completed. State-of-art computer system. Dining room now smoke-free. |
| 1992 | Renovations to eighteen rooms in North Lodge. Walk-in bay picture windows. New chef's cottage. Lake Rosseau Club renovated. Sundeck rebuilt. Cheltonia Cottage renovated. |
| 1992 | David Cornell marries Karen Harrington |
| 1993 | New ceiling for barbecue pavilion. Fairway cottage refurbished. |
| 1994 | Renovations to balance of North Lodge. New basketball court and nets. New kitchen added to barbecue pavilion. Telephones and double jack installations for computers in all accommodation. |
| 1995 | State-of-art fitness centre. Segwun Room addition to dining room. Can accommodate 540 guests in dining room. |
| 1996 | Two more kiddies pools. Tennis courts resurfaced. |
| 1997 | Clevelands House website. Total of 250 staff when open in the summer. |
| 1999 | Four new Bayview Suites. Verandah addition to Lakeside dining room. Thirty-foot extension to dock. Expansion of barbecue pavilion (Sagamo Centre) to incorporate banquet kitchen and bar. New 35-person hot tub. North Lodge common room renovated. Sixth tee of golf course relocated. |
| 2000 | Purchased 88 acres of adjoining land from Jim Minett. Three new Gardenview Suites. Redesigned Play World anchored by Cleve's Fun Ship. Expansion and relocation of fourth hole of golf course. Time capsule buried on Thanksgiving weekend, to be re-opened on Saturday, May 21 2050. New history book researched by Susan Pryke. |

# Bibliography

## Books

Boyer, Barbaranne. *Muskoka's Grand Hotels*. Erin: Boston Mills Press, 1987.

Cameron, Taylor. *Enchanted Summers: The Grand Hotels of Muskoka*. Toronto: Lynx Images, 1997.

Coombe, Geraldine. *Muskoka Past and Present*. Toronto: McGraw-Hill Ryerson Ltd., 1976.

Cumberland, Barlow, ed. *Muskoka and the Northern Lakes of Canada*. Toronto: Hunter, Rose and Company, 1886.

Duke, A. H. and Gray, W. M. *The Boatbuilders of Muskoka*. Erin: Boston Mills Press, 1992.

Hosking, Carol. *Clevelands House: Summer Memories*. Erin: Boston Mills Press, 1988.

Jocque, Violet. *Pioneers and Latecomers*. Minett, 1979

King, Harriet. *Letter From Muskoka by An Emigrant Lady*. London: Richard Bentley and Son, 1878. (Published anonymously.)

Muskoka Lakes *Blue Book Directory and Chart*, 1918.

Pryke, Susan. *Explore Muskoka*. Erin: Boston Mills Press, 1987. Revised edition 1999.

Pryke, Susan. *Explore Muskoka Lakes*. Erin: Boston Mills Press, 1990.

*Summertimes*. Erin: Boston Mills Press, 1994.

Tatley, Richard. *The Steamboat Era in the Muskokas*. 2 vols. Erin: Boston Mills Press, 1983, 1984.

## Manuscripts and diaries

Ames, Mabel Croucher. "The Founding of Craigie Lea and Carlingford House, Lake Joseph, Muskoka." Typed manuscript, 1975.

Henry, Betty. "Diary of the Henry Family." Typed manuscript, 2000.

Linney, Harry. "Summer Days: Boats are Everywhere." Typed manuscript, 1928.

Minett, Bill. "The History of Clevelands House." (n.d)

*Peninsula Women's Institute Tweedsmuir History.*

Penson, Seymour Richard George. "Memoirs." Typed manuscript, 1910.

Troup, Margaret, Bonythyn, Mary (pseudonym). "The Juddhaven Story." Typed manuscript, 1946.

*Sanford Women's Institute Tweedsmuir History.*

## Atlases

*Guide Book and Atlas of Muskoka and Parry Sound Districts*, 1879.

*Map and Chart of the Muskoka Lakes*, 1899.

## Records

Census of Canada records

Census of Gloucestershire County (England)

Church of Jesus Christ of Latter Day Saints Genealogy Library, Bracebridge

Corporation of the United Townships of Medora and Wood minutes

Medora Township papers, MS 658 reel 294, 295, Archives of Ontario,

Muskoka Lakes Museum Collection

Registry office files

## Newspapers and newsletters

*Bracebridge Gazette*
*Bracebridge Herald*
*Bracebridge Herald-Gazette*
*Huntsville Forester*
*Muskokan*
*Muskoka Sun*
*Northern Advocate*
*Toronto World*
*Clevelands House newsletters*

# Index

96